JOHN WELCH

THE MAN WHO
COULDN'T BE STOPPED

D1638206

JOHN WELCH

THE MAN WHO
COULDN'T BE STOPPED

ETHEL BARRETT

CHRISTIAN FOCUS

© Copyright 2004 Ethell Barrett
ISBN 1-85792- 9284
Published IN 2004
by
Christian Focus Publications,
Geanies House, Fearn,
Ross-shire, IV20 1TW,
Great Britain

Life summary sections,
What was life like then?
and *John Welch Time Line*
© Copyright 2004
Christian Focus Publications

Cover design by Alister Macinnes
Cover illustration by Fred Apps
Maps by Stuart Mingham.

Printed and bound in Great Britain by
Cox and Wyman Ltd, Reading, Berkshire

Contents

WHO'S IN CHARGE HERE?

Such hugger-muggery! Yes, it's a word, all right; it's in the dictionary. And it means *confusion*. Back in the sixteen hundreds, the Christian world was in the grip of hugger-muggery almost beyond belief.

Those Catholics! What they did to the Protestants! They destroyed their churches and disrupted their services and ambushed their leaders and even snatched away their children to be raised Catholics.

And those Protestants! What they did to the Catholics! They burned their monasteries and destroyed their churches and even broke into their services and snatched away their priests!

So those Catholics hugger-muggered those Protestants. And the Protestants hugger-muggered the Catholics. Who was in charge here? Who indeed? That's what the total confusion was all about.

This is the story of a boy who lived in this world of confusion, and who ran away from home to look for heroic adventure. He found what he was looking for, all right – but it was not until he changed his mind and went back home that his most exciting adventures began. When he grew to be a man, he found the most exciting adventures of all – beyond anything in his wildest boyhood dreams.

– In battles and hair-raising escapes. With robbers and kings and sinners and saints. In bravery and treachery – and love.

God gave him everything he was looking for – and a great deal more.

This book is based on his story – the true story of John Welch, one of the greatest Christian heroes in the 1600s.

A GOOD NIGHT
TO RUN AWAY

This would be a good night to run away. The fog was thick.

Johnny looked out his bedroom window. He knew that outside were the gardens, and beyond them the stone walls that surrounded his father's huge house, and beyond the walls, the green hills of Scotland. He smelled the clover, wet and fragrant, and the new-mown grass. Though he could see none of it through the fog, he smelled it and he felt it. He had planned this for a long, long time. For Johnny belonged to what was known as a "God-fearing" family, and he was weary of the rules that went along with it.

He was weary of going to church, and of being "preached at" at home. For years now, he had been skipping school whenever he could get away with it, and had spent his days wandering through the damp woods, lying on his stomach beside a stream, staring into the water at the fish – and dreaming. How wonderful it would be to get away, far away, and actually see a city – a big city - and to live a life of undreamed-of adventure, so that everyone who knew of him would say, 'Ahhh, Johnny Welch – there's a lad who's not afraid of anybody!'

Anybody?

The truth was, Johnny was dreadfully afraid of his own father. His father was the lord of the manor house – wealthy, respected in the neighbourhood – and very, very stern, with piercing eyes and a beard that seemed as long as a yardstick. Johnny stood by the window and shivered at the very thought of him. He had to run away. He was nearly fourteen; it was time to do it. He had to do it tonight.

He turned from the window and went back to his bed where he had his clothes all carefully laid out along with a leather flask for water, and a large plaid shawl spread out flat to put his few provisions in. He dressed hurriedly, trembling in the dark; he did not dare light a candle.

Moments later he opened his door carefully and stepped outside. He started down the hall past his father's bedroom. His father was snoring.

He started down the steps. And stopped. They creaked. He tested each step after that, wondering why he'd never noticed before that they creaked. At last he was safely at the bottom. He started across the enormous living room, past the huge stone fireplace and into the kitchen, where the oatmeal was slowly bubbling on the back of the kitchen stove for the morning's breakfast. He very carefully took the cover off the huge cauldron and laid it alongside. Then he tiptoed to the cupboard and brought back a bowl. He ladled a big glop of oatmeal into it and set it on the table. He put the cover back on the cauldron and tiptoed into the pantry. He scooped up all he could find – some biscuits, a jar of honey, some cheese. He skipped the butter and the cream. He could not carry them, and besides the butter would melt and the cream would curdle in the heat of the day. He tiptoed back out to the kitchen and gulped down the oatmeal. Then he spread his shawl out on the table, put his provisions in, and tied it up. He went toward the back door, undid the lock, and started to open it – and stopped.

It creaked too, louder than the stairs had. He had never noticed it before. In the daytime he'd never heard it creak; why did it have to creak now? He pulled it a little farther.

Creeeeak. He listened, his hands trembling. Was his father still snoring? He was too far away to hear. Right now, Johnny was more afraid of his father than he was of God.

He got it open just wide enough to slip through, and then ever so carefully – *creeeak* – he closed it. Outside, the fog was so thick he could scarcely see, but he could smell the pungent odour of his mother's herb garden near the kitchen. His mother loved herbs. The food on their table was always fragrant with them.

He paused, thinking of his mother. She was a quiet little woman who had never, to his knowledge, spoken back to his father. Nobody every spoke back to his father. His piercing eyes and bristling beard frightened everyone about him into silence. But his mother. She would be broken-hearted that he would turn his back on everything he had been taught from his childhood – that he would actually run away. She would cry. His father would be angry. He would storm about and rant and rave and disown Johnny forever.

Johnny closed the door softly behind him and walked down the path that ran through the middle of the herb garden. He could think *behind*; he must think *ahead*. He walked past the herb garden, through the lawns and shrubbery beyond, down to the gate. He didn't need to see; he knew every step by heart. The dogs lying by the outside gate whimpered as he drew near, but they did not bark.

'Quiet,' he whispered, and he petted them one by one. 'Quiet. It's all right. It's all right.' They wagged and whined and he shushed them again. He opened the huge gate and closed it softly behind him.

He was on the road at last. He fancied he heard his father snoring even from this distance. At any moment his father would waken, snort, and leap out of bed and come bellowing to the window, like some giant in a nightmare, to order him back.

But none of this happened. Everything was silent. He sighed with relief and started nimbly down the road through the blanket of fog. He knew every rut, every turn, every inch of it by heart.

He covered the first mile easily, sometimes running, on to his freedom. Then he settled down to a walk, past all the sights of his boyhood, past the sign *TO DUMFRIES* that led to his Aunt Agnes's house.

Aunt Agnes had always made him think of a sparrow in her plain grey dresses, bobbing about and chirping. He thought of her house, rambling and comfortable, set in the midst of a garden, beautiful beyond words, with her herb garden outside her kitchen, and flowers everywhere else, right up to the stone wall that surrounded it. He stopped a moment by the sign and leaned against it. He loved his Aunt Agnes. For a moment he thought of side-tracking, just to stand outside her house. He was sure he wouldn't hear her snore. Aunt Agnes just wouldn't snore.

He sighed, and then trudged on down the main road. He hated to leave Aunt Agnes; he hated to leave his mother. But he had to go. He had to get away from his father. He had to get away from school. He had to get away from all the things that held him back and fenced him in and bound him down. All the rules, rules, endless rules. He had to get away from the rules.

He walked with new determination, into the foggy night.

*   *   *

The sun was shining through the fog when Johnny awoke. At first he didn't realize where he was. He had trudged through the fog all night, not daring to stop, until the black night had turned to grey, and then, unable to keep on his feet any longer, he had crawled into some bush by the side of the road and fallen asleep at once.

He struggled to a sitting position, stiff and damp, and opened his shawl. He chose a biscuit and munched it slowly. He must not eat too fast – he had to make it last. When he was finished, he got up cautiously, looking about him for any sign of life. He was halfway to his feet when he stopped suddenly, his blood frozen.

There was a rustle in the grass.

He waited, motionless, hardly daring to breathe, and then let out a long sigh of relief, blowing through his mouth.

A rabbit! It scampered by, less than two feet from him, and ran for its life. *He's more scared than I am*, Johnny thought, breathing hard. And then, very cautiously, he tied up his shawl and stepped out onto the road.

There was no sign of life anywhere, no one in the fields as far as he could see. Stone wall fences stretched out in the distance, but he could see no sign of a house or a barn. He started trudging down the road. The worst was over, he thought. He'd be all right now. He was far enough away from neighbours – wait a minute.

The clop-clop of horses' hoofs, slow and heavy – work horses, probably. Were they ahead? No. He looked back. They were behind, off in the distance. His guess had been right. It was a huge wagon pulled by work horses, slow and plodding, saving energy for the hot day ahead. He turned and walked again, staring straight before him. All his muscles strained to send him flying into the bushes. His reflexes said *run*, but his mind said *no*, and he forced himself to keep trudging up the road, looking straight ahead. What if it was a neighbour? Or someone who knew his father? His blood ran cold at the thought. *Maybe he'll pass me by*, he thought, *maybe he'll go on.*

'Make him go on, dear God,' he muttered under his breath, 'make him go on,' forgetting that it was his parents' godly life that had made him run away from God in the first place. 'Make him go on –' He kept muttering it right up until the clop-clop got slower, and then stopped.

'Where are you going?' a rough voice called. John forced himself to turn. Where was he going? He didn't even know where he *was*.

'Ah – just down to the – next – just down a way,' he stammered, as he looked up into the gruff face of a farm-hand. The man was a stranger. *Thank God*, John thought.

'Climb up,' the man said, indicating his high seat. But John sprang nimbly into the wagon behind him instead. That way he wouldn't have to talk. The man clicked to his horses, and they started slowly onward. John scrunched down in the wagon, his back to the man.

'Going any place in particular?' the man called over his shoulder.

'Going to visit my Aunt Agnes,' Johnny lied. Aunt Agnes was snug in her little cottage, many miles behind, but it was all he could think of to say. 'She lives – a long way down, a long way from here.' He did not dare to name a town. To his relief the man said no more. The loud rumble of the wheels and the clop of the horses' hoofs drowned out all further attempts at conversation. He rode on for what seemed like forever, looking backwards at the road stretching out behind. Every mile was taking him farther and farther away from his father.

It was early afternoon before the man pulled his horses to a stop. 'Got to drop you off here, lad,' the rough voice called back. 'I'm turning off.'

John scrambled off the wagon and muttered his thanks. The man nodded and turned to the left. John stood there a moment, stretching his cramped muscles, and then started stiffly on down the road. The day was hot now, but his spirits were still not dampened. He was on his way to freedom.

Throughout the rest of the long day he did not stop when he wanted to, only when he had to, out of hunger or sheer exhaustion. When night came he scrambled off the road and into the bushes again. He sank down and opened his shawl. He ate sparingly and forced himself only a little of his precious water. Then he sank gratefully into sleep. It was a sleep filled with hobgoblins he'd dreamed of as a little child. But when he awoke in the morning, the dreams vanished and he realized suddenly that much of his fear had gone. After all, he had survived that first scary day. The man in the wagon had swallowed his story about visiting Aunt Agnes without blinking. Lying to strangers was easy, he thought; they had no reason not to believe you, or else they did not care. The trick was to talk as little as possible and if anyone persisted with questions, just use the story of Aunt Agnes again.

* * *

Days later Johnny was still going south. By now he was not bounding along, or even trudging; he was staggering. He got rides from one farm to the next and sank down by the roadside at night to sleep. He had no idea how far he had gone. His meagre supplies had given out. He travelled as far as he could as long as he could see, but each night, earlier and earlier, the fog settled in and he curled up to sleep.

And then one night he saw the campfire up in the hills. People by now were snuggled safely in their cottages, the candles lit. He sank back beside the road, looking up at the campfire in the distance. He was so hungry he was wobbly. He had to make a decision. He could either wait and try to hitch a ride in the morning, or he could go up to that campfire.

He rested awhile, then stood up and crossed the road. He plunged into the bushes and started up the hill.

It took him an hour to get up there, and by that time he was so ravenously hungry he could hardly stand. He crept up to about a hundred yards from the campfire, crouched in the bushes, and watched. Beside the campfire were the remains of a sheep that had been butchered and dismembered. Around the campfire was a group of men chewing on huge chunks of the lamb that they had roasted over the fire.

And their faces were more terrifying than his father's face had ever been!

They were grizzled and worn. And their eyes – not the stern eyes of his father. They were something else – what were they? They were cold and unfeeling. They were *evil*.

He crouched there staring at them, half in fear, half in amazement. And then one of them looked up and saw him.

'Well,' he cried, chewing on a leg of lamb, 'and who have we here?' They all looked at him, staring suspiciously.

'Who are you, lad?' another one said.

'What's your name?'

'My name is Johnny,' he began, and then stopped. Obviously, Johnny could no longer be his name if he was going to embark on a life of adventure. 'My name is John,' he said as forcefully as he could. 'And I'm hungry.'

They looked him over. 'Look at 'im,' another one said. 'A mere stripling of a lad. Still has peach fuzz on his face.' They roared at this. Johnny took a step forward to show them just how brave he was, but his knees buckled and he fell. 'I'm hungry,' he said again.

'And look at the fine clothes the lad has,' another said. 'From a rich father, no doubt.' And he threw Johnny a piece of meat. Johnny caught it easily and began to eat as he'd never eaten before. He chewed away at the meat until he got down to the bone. Then he laid the bone on his trembling knees and sat on his heels.

'What d'you want, lad?' the first one said, 'Come here to spy on us?'

'No,' John said impulsively, 'I came to join

you.'

They roared again.

'Join us!' They said, 'Well you've got a lot to learn, lad. But no mind. We'll teach you. Come on over.'

He crept forward and joined their circle. And that night he learned to laugh when they laughed, though he could not see what was funny. And when they fell silent, he learned to keep his mouth closed. Before the night was far spent, he learned from their talking that he had joined a band of thieves. Well, wasn't this, after all, adventure?

Wasn't this what he had been looking for? And wasn't all this why he had run away?

He curled up beside the fire, too exhausted to even think about it. Except for one little twinge, just before he fell asleep. It was just about the hour when family prayers would be said back home. Would they be praying for his safety? He pushed away a feeling of guilt. He would not think of it. After all, he had, at long last, reached his goal, his heart's desire. He'd run away from his father.

He was free!

What he did not realize was that he had also run away from God.

GRADUATE THIEF

John awakened to the sound of a distant screech owl and the soft chill of a mountain breeze. Midges buzzed in his ear, annoyingly itching his skin as he turned over sleepily and then realized he was not in his bed at home; he was on the hard ground and every muscle in his body ached. He groaned, clasped his hands under his head, and opened one eye. The fire was out but there was a buttery moon overhead and in its light he could see that the men were gone except for one – a short squat man whose name he'd forgotten. 'They've all gone down the hill to the village,' the man answered Johnny's unspoken question. 'We do our stealin' at night.'

Johnny got up painfully on one elbow.

'My name's Mac,' the man went on. 'We don't get fancy with last names around here.'

'My name's John,' Johnny said, in case the man had forgotten it.

'John is it?' The man laughed. 'Now ain't that grown up? I think I'll call you Johnny-boy. You're a mere stripling of a lad.'

Johnny blushed in the dark. 'Just exactly where is this?' he asked, trying to sound grown-up.

'We're at the border of Scotland and England,' Mac said, staring hard at Johnny and sucking his teeth. He was grinning though; he was still amused, and Johnny had the uncomfortable feeling that he was being laughed at. 'From here we can rob the villages from both countries. This way we're not partial,' Mac added, and laughed hard at his own joke. 'No sir, you can't say we're partial,' he said again when he'd finished laughing.

'Can I –' Johnny began.

'Sure, if you want to fall in with us,' Mac said quickly. 'But you've got to do your share.

You can't hang around here for nothing. But don't worry about it. I'll teach you the tricks.'

Johnny grinned bashfully, excited over being included in this adventure. 'You can come along with me for a while until you learn,' Mac went on. 'And a good help you'll be, too. For you're nice and skinny. You can squeeze in spaces where I can't.'

Johnny's grin wobbled a bit at this; it was not quite so flattering to realize he was wanted only because he was skinny.

'Back to sleep,' Mac said, 'You can sleep tomorrow, too, if you like. You'll start work in earnest tomorrow night.'

As it turned out, it was two weeks or more before Johnny "started work in earnest." He went to the village with Mac night after night, watching and listening as Mac taught him how to break into a house and steal. He paid far more attention to Mac than he had ever paid to any teacher back in school.

When Mac decided that he had "graduated" and was finally ready to rob a house on his own, Johnny could hardly contain his excitement. When the night came, and he stood in front of the house Mac had picked for him to rob, he couldn't believe he was finally there. He could not remember at all how he had got down from the hills. All he could remember was Mac's frequent, 'Stop jabbering, lad, you'll talk your jaw off.' He stood in the bushes with Mac, trembling with excitement. All he knew was that he'd somehow got there, and that the great adventure was about to begin.

'Nobody home here,' Mac said, and he gestured toward the windows on the dark side of the house. 'Been watching this house for a week. Try the windows at that end. If they're locked, don't bother with them. Come back. And stay in the shadows.' He gave Johnny a gentle push. 'Off with you, lad,' he said.

Johnny darted away, staying out of the moonlight, and got to the first window shaking with a mixture of anticipation and fright. He probed under the bottoms of the shutters with his fingers. They gave instantly under his pressure, and he pulled them outward without any trouble. He pushed carefully on the casement windows behind. They opened easily. He pushed them inward and then stretched his arms in and felt the wide sill inside to make sure there was nothing on it. He hiked himself up and slid carefully across the sill and eased himself down to the floor.

A path of moonlight shot across the room from the open window. He could see the room easily. The light caught the glow of silver candlesticks on the mantel. Then he saw the glow of silver from the various tables about the room. Suddenly his fear was gone and a feeling of self-confidence, even cockiness, swept over him. He untied his sack from around his waist and walked over to the mantel, the bottom of his sack dragging on the floor. He reached for the candlesticks, but suddenly – the long muscles in his arms that were supposed to coordinate his movements refused to behave. His arm shot out, crashed into the candlesticks, and sent them clattering to the floor. A plate standing upright behind them came tumbling down with a "ping" and spun like a coin, round and round on the stone hearth, then fell on its bottom and wobbled noisily before it finally came to a stop. He stared, horrified, forgetting for a moment that the house was empty. Then he chuckled nervously to himself. Phew. And then –

He stopped. His breath caught in his throat. There was a scuffling noise upstairs. Somebody was in the house.

Suddenly he had an almost overpowering urge to cry out to Mac, '*Help. Somebody is in the house!*'

He bit his tongue and choked it back. Now his whole being was one bundle of pure panic, he turned and lunged toward the window, stepping clumsily into his sack with one foot. It got caught between his feet as he struggled to get out of it. He leaped at the broad window sill and slid across it as if both he and it were greased. He shot out of the window like one of the apple seeds he used to squeeze between thumb and finger and send flying into the air. He landed on all fours and ran, hardly touching the ground, toward the bushes. He threw himself forward headlong, gasping and sobbing, into Mac's waiting arms. Mac bunched his sack against his mouth and boxed him on the head so hard his ears rang. It was a not-so-gentle reminder to be silent and Johnny obeyed instantly, swallowing his sobs with difficulty until they dissolved into hiccups.

'You've got oatmeal for a brain, lad,' Mac muttered, shaking his head.

They made their retreat in silence, looking back over their shoulders every few steps until at last it was apparent that they were safe. 'You've got oatmeal for a brain,' Mac said again. Johnny didn't answer. They went the rest of the way in silence, until they got to the top of the hill, and made their way to the fire.

Some of the men straggled in. They looked at Mac, their eyes questioning. 'There was somebody in the house,' he said. 'But the lad escaped. He came flying out of the window like a bloomin' cannonball.'

They all laughed at this, as Mac half steered, half dragged, Johnny over to an empty space and tossed him down beside the fire like a gunnysack. Johnny landed with a thud. Someone threw a biscuit and a piece of meat in his direction. He did not want it. He rolled over on his face.

The last thing he heard before he fell asleep was Mac's voice, 'He came flying out like a bloomin' cannonball!' And the men's uproarious laughter.

* * *

Through the following weeks and months John learned, under Mac's watchful eye, all the tricks of stealing, until finally they let him operate alone.

During most of the day he slept. During the night he took his sack and sneaked stealthily down the hill – down to the houses of the wealthy on the other side of the border. He learned what to steal – silver candlesticks, heirlooms, whatever he could find that was of value – and, of course, money. And when his sack was full, like a worker-bee with his pollen bags full, he made his way back up into the hills to the campsite. He ate what he could manage to grab, and listened to the rough talk of the men. They had accepted him now as one of them.

As the months went by his peach fuzz turned to stubble. He thought about his new life as he curled up by the fire each night. This was freedom. Of course, everything he stole got turned over to the leaders of the band. And there were times when he had a sneaking feeling that God was looking over his shoulder. But at least he was away from his father.

Every day he slept. And every night he went out to steal again. And every day he slept. And every night he went out to steal again and every day he slept again.

This was freedom?

The fine suit of clothes he'd worn when he'd left his father's house was in tatters. His pants were held up by a rope. Except for being filled with food every night he was more desolate than he'd ever been in his father's house. Where was the adventure? Where was the freedom?

It took a year.

One night he stumbled back up through the bushes, his sack full of loot, and dumped it before the band of leaders. He sat by the campfire and devoured his share of food and listened to the talk. And thought.

He thought hard. That was the night he suddenly fancied he smelled the fragrant herbs from his mother's kitchen garden. And her delicious food. And the bubbling of the porridge on the back of the kitchen stove. He smelled the fragrance of the big garden and the sweet new-mown grass. He saw the long clean furrows plowed in the fields beyond. He saw, for a moment, his father's stern eyes –

That stopped him for a moment, but he dreamed on. He thought of all the opportunities he'd had to learn at school and all the times he'd played hooky. And for one brief second he felt sorrow like a little "ping" that he had not finished his schooling. He thought of his good clothing, cool in the summer, warm and snug in the winter – always just right. And of all the provisions his father had made for him. And yes, for a moment, he thought of his father kneeling during family prayer time. He sat bolt upright there at the campfire and looked at all the evil faces around it. And then it came full-blown into his mind.

This is *freedom*?

He curled up by the fire and slept. That evening he sat at supper saying nothing. He listened to their evil chatter without hearing. He did his night's work, then slept through the next day.

That night as they went off to steal he hung behind. 'Comin, lad?' they called.

'Be right with you,' he called back. 'In a minute; I can't find my sack.' And he busied himself, pretending to look for the sack that he had kicked under a bush. The rest of the men started down the hillside, but Mac held back. Johnny straightened up and looked at him for a moment.

'You all right?' Mac called.

'Yes,' Johnny said, but his heart began to beat faster. Had he said it too quickly? Did Mac suspect? He turned again and raked the ground with his feet, swishing brush and twigs aside, pretending to look for the sack. He forced himself to keep looking down as if he were unaware of Mac watching him. It was a long time before he felt sure that Mac was gone. He walked over to the bush where he had hidden the sack; he was slow and cautious, ready to change his course at a second's notice if anyone was watching him. Then, still slow and cautious, he got it out from under the bush. He went back to the fire, gathered up what food he could, and dumped it in his sack. He hitched up his pants that were tied with a rope, plunged into the bushes, and headed down the other side of the hill.

He was going back to his father.

Back to his *father*? He thought about it as he hurried down the hillside. The long trek home was going to be a hard one, maybe impossible. A hard one, a hard one, kept drumming through his head, as he trudged along the road. He stopped when he was no longer able to stand, chewed on a few scraps of meat, and trudged on.

'Going north?' he would call out to every passing farmer, brave now, more sure of himself. "Going north," the farmer would answer and stop his wagon, and take him a few more miles up the road. And so the long hard journey began. He either rode or stumbled along the roads by day, and slept in the fog at night. His home, he thought, his home, his home, his mother – his father –

His father? His father would cut him up in little pieces too short to hang up. His father – with the piercing eyes and the beard as long as a yardstick. Would he soften a bit if Johnny told him he wanted to go back to school?

Even as he thought it, he realized that he *did* want to go back. Would his father believe him? What would he say? Or Aunt Agnes? Suppose he talked to her first? She had a way with people. She had a way with his father.

It was the very next day that he spotted the sign *TO DUMFRIES* that led to his Aunt Agnes's house. Dared he go there? Dared he?

A TRAMP COMES TO TEA

Miss Agnes Forsythe of Dumfries was a tiny woman. She flitted about like a bird, scolding her servants, but she always chirped when she did it and they loved her. As Johnny had said, she had a way with people. Though she seldom talked about her nephew (his father had forbidden it) she had never ceased to pray for him.

This particular day her house was bustling as usual; the servants were about their business, dinner was cooking in the kitchen, and afternoon tea was ready to serve. It was just like any other afternoon. Settled in her front parlour she waited for her parlourmaid Annie to bring in her tea. But when Annie came into the room, she had no tea tray. Instead she stumbled in, breathing hard, rubbing her hands up and down on her long white starched apron. She was bristling with excitement.

'What is it, Annie?' Miss Agnes said.

'Miss Forsythe,' Annie said with the air of someone about to make an earthshaking announcement, 'there's a beggar at the back door.'

'Well, indeed,' said Miss Agnes, 'give him something to eat and send him on his way.'

'But he says he knows you,' Annie persisted, nearly bursting with importance. 'He says he's your *nephew*. But he doesn't look like –'

Miss Agnes started up from her settee, looking at Annie in unbelief, 'He says he's my nephew?' she repeated. 'Are you sure?'

Annie nodded her head in little frightened jerks. 'But he doesn't look at all like –' she tried again.

Miss Agnes started for the door. There was nothing bird-like about her now. 'If he says he's my nephew,' she said, 'I shall go and see him at once.'

'But Miss Agnes,' Annie persisted, 'he has stubble all over his face. His trousers are held up by a rope. He doesn't *look* like your nephew. He looks like a tramp.'

'So a tramp he might be,' Aunt Agnes said, 'but if he says he's my nephew, then he must at least know something about me. At any rate I've got to see him – to talk to him.' She quickened her steps and trotted down the hall toward the back door. It was closed and bolted. Annie was cautious.

'I've got to see for myself,' muttered Aunt Agnes again, this time to herself. She unbolted the door and opened it.

There before her stood the beggar, his peach fuzz grown into the beginnings of a beard. 'Miss Agnes,' he began, and then, 'Auntie – auntie.'

She stood there a moment, aghast, and then – 'Johnny, *Johnny*!'

'Auntie,' the stranger said again, 'I've come home.'

Aunt Agnes was a woman of no nonsense. She did not waste words.

'Come in,' she said, 'into the front parlour. I'm just about to have tea.'

Annie appeared at her shoulder. 'But Miss *Forsythe*,' she warbled, 'surely you can't –'

'Surely I *can*,' said Miss Agnes matter-of-factly. 'This is my nephew. We're going to have tea – in the front parlour.'

'But, Aunt Agnes,' John began, 'I'm dirty.'

'He's dirty,' Annie said at the same time.

'In my front parlour,' Miss Forsythe said again. 'Come in, Johnny,' and she bustled down the hall. 'It's just like old times. Annie, bring scones and anything else you can think of. This lad must be hungry.'

Annie was aghast.

John was terrified.

But Aunt Agnes was triumphant. She settled herself on her best settee and motioned John to sit beside her. 'Now Johnny,' she said, as if he'd just been there a week ago, 'tell me what's up. What's the news?'

And before he had a chance to answer, she hurried on – 'Bless us, your peach fuzz is turning into a beard. Tell me what's happened to you. Tell me everything,' she said as if they were conspirators about to share an adventure.

Annie brought in the tea and scones and some sandwiches, and retreated, after glaring at John with suspicion.

John sat there, running his hand over his beginning beard, not knowing where to begin.

'Aunt Agnes,' he started, 'I've come back –'

'So I see,' she said tartly, 'have a scone. And a sandwich. Have a handful. You must be starved.'

He grabbed a fistful and devoured them all hungrily.

'Take them all,' she said. 'I eat too much anyway. Now tell me.'

And John told her. He told her everything, not sparing himself. And at the end – 'I want to go back to my father,' he said.

'Well of course you do,' she said matter-of-factly, 'You want to come back to all of us.

That's natural. I've been praying for you for a year.'

'But I'm afraid of him,' he said desperately. 'Would you – do you suppose you could – speak to him for me? Go to him first and explain? And ask him if he would see me?'

'Well of course I will,' she said. 'What makes you think I wouldn't? The point is, we have to take first things first. We have to decide just what to do and how to do it.'

Then they both stopped talking and listened. There was a clatter of wheels and horses' hoofs outside the window. John sprang up and bolted for the door to the back parlour.

'Now wait a minute!' Aunt Agnes said. 'I know it's not your father. It can't be. He never comes to see me on Wednesday, he always comes on Thursdays. So just hold it!' And she picked up her skirts and hurried to the window, chattering all the while. 'I know it's not your father.' She pulled the drapes aside. 'It just can't be – oh my word, Johnny. It *is* your father. And I can handle him.'

She pushed him toward a closet.

'In,' she said, pulling some drapes aside and shoving him past clothes and boxes to the back wall. 'Back!' she ordered, 'and stop trembling. You're shaking the drapes. Dead giveaway.'

He scrunched inside as best he could and she pulled the drapes closed. 'Johnny, stop shaking,' she said again, backing out of the room toward the hall. 'I'll handle your father. Just leave him to me.'

A moment later, John heard their voices out in the hall. 'Well, John, I didn't expect you,' Aunt Agnes said to John's father. 'But it's a great pleasure. Come in. I was just having some tea.'

John flattened himself tighter against the closet wall and listened as they settled themselves. They went on, endlessly, it seemed, with small talk – and then, finally, Aunt Agnes's voice, saying what he'd been dreading. 'And have you heard anything from Johnny?'

John heard his father's tea cup clatter back to the saucer. Then his father's voice.

'Oh don't,' he said, and it came out like a moan. 'It is cruel. How can you even say his name to me? I'm afraid for him – I'm afraid for his very life. The first news I expect to hear is that he's been hanged as a thief.' And there was such sadness in his voice that Johnny would have slid to the floor if he had not been wedged between boxes in the closet; it was only the boxes that held him up.

By now Aunt Agnes was holding her cup with both hands. It was shaking so, she couldn't control it with one. 'Oh I don't know,' she said, trying to put her cup back into her saucer carefully and not succeeding. It landed halfway up on the saucer rim and stayed there, teetering. 'There's many a boy who's had a dark beginning and a very bright ending, dear brother.'

Johnny listened, hardly daring to breathe, as his father went on. 'Agnes,' he said, 'what are you trying to tell me? Is it possible that you've had some news of him? Do you know where he is? Oh, if I only knew he was even alive!'

John waited in the silence. Then he heard Aunt Agnes's voice again. 'Johnny!' she called, and her voice was shrill with nervousness. 'Come out here!'

John pushed the drapes aside, took one step into the parlour – and stopped, trembling. His father had gotten to his feet and was staring at him as if he were seeing a ghost. And then Aunt Agnes found her tongue. 'Here's Johnny!' she cried in a high tremolo that almost ended in a giggle. 'He's come home, John.'

John stared at his father. His beard was dark and pointed, but not as long as a yardstick, the way Johnny had imagined. He had suddenly become the stern parent again, looking as fierce as ever. But somehow not as frightening now. For John had heard his heartbroken voice. Why, his father really loved him!

John took another step toward his father, and then fell to his knees. 'Father,' he said, 'I've come home to ask you to forgive me.'

'What!?!' his father bellowed.

'For Jesus' sake,' John said, remembering the prayers of his boyhood. And then all the things he'd planned to say, all the things he felt in his heart, came pouring out at once, his words tumbling over each other. 'I know I've disgraced you, Father. I know I've broken your heart. But everything I ever did wrong, I always felt that God was looking over my shoulder, that he was after me, to bring me back. And I want to come back. I want to go back to school, Father – please.'

'Why?' his father said, but more softly now. 'You didn't finish grammar school. You skipped most of your classes. Why do you want to go back? What do you suppose you want to be?'

And then suddenly it came into John's mind. 'I want to be a minister,' he said.

Aunt Agnes sat down suddenly on her rose

settee. His father seemed to leave the floor a foot beneath him. "A *minister*?" he roared. 'And what right do *you* have to become a minister?'

But John's mind was straightened out at last. 'I want to go back to school. And I want to study to be a minister,' he said. 'Will you support me? Will you *help* me? Please?'

His father sat down suddenly, as if he'd been shot.

John knelt there, quiet. Aunt Agnes sank farther into the settee, trembling, waiting for her brother's reply.

There was a long silence.

And then, 'All right,' Mr Welch said at last.

They waited as if they were waiting for the end of the world.

'I'll send you back to school,' he said. 'I'll let you finish your education. We'll talk about the rest later. Don't make promises you can't keep.' And he started out of the room. At the door, he turned. 'But mind you,' he said, 'you must get good marks – the *top* marks – or I'm through with you forever. Do you understand?'

John staggered to his feet. 'I understand, father, he said quietly. 'If I don't keep my part of the bargain, you can – you can disown me.'

His father started across the hall.

'And Mother?' John asked, following him.

His father turned, his hand on the outside knob. 'Your mother will be very happy to know that you are back home,' he said, and a note of tenderness crept into his voice. And then, as if he was ashamed to be caught with his guard down, he became the stern parent again. 'Well?!!?' he said gruffly, his beard quivering, 'are you coming? I don't have all day.'

John looked at Aunt Agnes. She nodded. 'I'm coming, Father,' John said.

He already fancied he could smell his mother's herb garden outside her kitchen window.

ELIZABETH

John drove his buggy up to the brow of a hill overlooking the little town of Selkirk, and pulled his two fine Hackneys to a halt.

In the days that had followed his return home, his father had put him back in school. Then on to the college at Edinburgh. And John had listened to his teachers with the same enthusiasm and expectation that he had once listened to Mac's instructions on how to steal. All the foolishness had been drained out of him as if he'd pulled a plug in a bathtub. And now, seven years later, his man's beard trimmed and fashionable, he was, at long last, as he had promised his father – a minister!

He leaned forward in the buggy seat and

looked down at the little town of Selkirk. Its stone cottages seemed to huddle together as if they were afraid to stray away. The farms spread out in all directions, surrounded by stone walls. It was late autumn; the harvest had passed. Where there had been fields of grain and corn, there was just stubble. The trees that had been ablaze with colour only a few weeks before were mostly bare now, and a thin coating of frost covered the earth.

John's feet were wrapped in a blanket, and he had a plaid shawl draped over his heavy coat to keep warm. His nose was blue with cold, but his eyes were sparkling. This would be his first pastorate. He was a minister at last!

His horses snorted and tossed their heads and pawed the ground; he could see their breath in the cold air – his own breath too, as he pulled his nose out of the plaid shawl where it had been nuzzled. The cold air stung his nose, and he thrust it back in the warm wool again. He picked up the reins and clucked to his horses. They pulled back on the road and started down the hill. He was on his way at last, to his first great adventure. He was going to be a minister in this beautiful little town.

A half hour later, though, as he drove into the town, he realized it was beautiful only from a distance. The cobblestone streets were lined with small squalid houses and taverns and shops. The gutters at the sides of the streets were filled with garbage and slops that had been thrown from the windows. The fact that it was frozen didn't help much; it still smelled terrible. John steered his horses carefully down the centre of the street. He wondered where his lodging was, and what kind of a man Mr Mitchelhill would be. And whom he could ask for directions. A friendly face, he thought, and looked around.

Then suddenly he realized that somebody was staring at him. It was a middle-aged man, tall and stern, his eyes piercing underneath heavy brows, almost as frightening as John's father used to seem to him. John pulled his horses to a halt. 'Can you direct me to –' he began.

'Are you the new preacher?' the man interrupted him.

'Yes,' John said. 'I'm looking for a Mr Mitchelhill. I'm supposed to lodge at his house.'

'He's been expecting you,' the man said, but without any sign of welcome in his voice.

John kept smiling, though it wasn't quite as easy now. 'Would you be kind enough to tell me where he lives?'

'Just follow the main road,' the man said. 'He lives on the edge of town.' And he turned on his heel and disappeared into a tavern. Not a word of welcome. Not even a nod.

John urged his horses on down the street. The chill that had already settled in his bones was now aiming for his spirits. The words of a psalm came into his mind – *The Lord is on my side; I will not fear: what can man do unto me*?* He swallowed his disappointment and went doggedly on.

A mile down the road he turned in the driveway of Mr Mitchelhill. As he was

*Psalm 118:6

unwrapping the blanket from his feet, Mitchelhill himself came running out the front door, followed by a boy of about fourteen. 'Jim!' he called to someone who came running from the barn. 'Come tether the horses. It's the new minister.' He called it again toward the house. 'It's the new minister!' Then he looked up at John. 'Well, Mr Welch, welcome to Selkirk.'

John climbed down from the buggy, stiff with cold, but grateful. Mr Mitchelhill, bless him, had a merry face. In fact, he looked as if smoke would curl up alongside from his old pipe like old St Nick.

'Come in the house and warm your hide, sir. This is my son Jamie.'

The boy thrust his hand out in greeting, and they both grinned.

'Mrs Mitchelhill!' Mitchelhill called to his wife, as they reached the house. 'It's the new minister. Come say hello!'

They were in the living room by this time. Mrs Mitchelhill came from the kitchen, with her little prim cap, her little prim walk – and a *very* prim face, just bordering on glum. 'Ah,' she said in surprise, but John knew better; he'd seen her peeking from the window. 'My, lad, you're real young,' she added.

Later, over a supper of Mrs Mitchelhill's lentil soup and huge slabs of cold mutton, he learned a little more about the town – all of it gloomy.

'I might as well tell you, Mr Welch,' his host said, 'you were called by only a few. Some of us merchants got together and called you here. You won't have much of a church. And as for your lodgings – well, you won't have a house of your own either. You'll have to room here with us. You won't even have a room of your own, lad. You'll have Jamie for a bedfellow.'

John looked across the table at Jamie, who was smiling back timidly. 'I'm happy to have Jamie for a roommate," he said. And then to Jamie, "That is, if you'll have me.'

'Oh yes, sir,' Jamie said.

'Jamie looks to me like a very good lad,' John said. 'I wish that I had been half as good when I was his age.'

'You're still very young,' Mrs Mitchelhill murmured doubtfully. 'Most of the people in town didn't want you.'

'Oh it wasn't *you* they didn't want,' Mitchelhill added quickly. 'They didn't want a *minister*.'

Good start, John thought. *If I had to name this town I wouldn't name it Selkirk. I'd name it Gloomstown.*

'Well, I know one gentleman who certainly didn't want me,' he said aloud. Mitchelhill raised his eyebrows in a question. 'I asked him for directions to your house,' John went on. 'He asked me if I was the new preacher, and when I told him yes, he gave me a look that would freeze your blood. He even looked at my horses with hatred. I suppose if they'd been sway-back and broken-down he would have felt better. Or perhaps he wanted me to shuffle into town on foot with my possessions in a knapsack slung over my shoulder.'

'That would be Scot of Headschaw,' Mitchelhill said. 'No, he didn't want a preacher at all. And the fact that you looked prosperous and came in a fine wagon with good horses didn't help any.'

'Why should he hate me?' John said. 'He doesn't even know me.'

'Aye, he hated you before you ever got here,' Mitchelhill said. 'Don't worry about it.'

John nodded, and they talked of other things. But he was uneasy.

My first church, John thought later as he undressed and crawled beneath the covers of the big featherbed. He blew out the candle and scrunched down into the warmth gratefully. Jamie was already asleep.

Mitchelhill had painted a gloomy picture; his first church was not going to be easy. But he had fine warm clothing, a good buggy, and two strong horses. His father had sent him off in style. So he'd get along somehow; he'd leave it with God.

He had an encouraging note from his father

in his trunk and one from his mother. And Aunt Agnes. And one from Elizabeth.

Elizabeth was a girl who lived in Edinburgh. John had met her when he was studying there. She was the daughter of John Knox, one of the most famous preachers in all of the British Isles. Knox was dead now, but his name was not dead; indeed he had left his memory trailing behind him like the tail of a flaming comet. Though he'd been born Catholic, he had turned Protestant and had become a bitter enemy of the Catholic queen – Mary, Queen of Scots. Now, all this had happened when Elizabeth was an infant, but no one had forgotten it – for Queen Mary had been the *mother* of the very king who was reigning now – King James!

So to this day the very word "Knox" was a fighting word to any Catholic!

John knew that he was a long way from being ready to have a wife. He also knew that if he married there was no way he could live life in a corner. But there was one more thing he knew. He couldn't get her off his mind. He was in love with her.

He drifted off to sleep as the clock struck ten, and dreamed of preaching, high up in a pulpit, looking down over his listeners, and at Elizabeth in the front row.

It was the clock striking two that awakened him. He sat up in bed, spread his plaid shawl around his shoulders, and began to pray. He poured out all his hopes and dreams. He talked to God as if he were in the very room.

An hour later he was still praying. It wasn't until Jamie scrambled up on one elbow that he remembered the boy was in bed with him. He turned his head in surprise. Jamie was looking at him as if he were a ghost. 'I'm sorry, Jamie,' he said. 'I didn't mean to wake you; I forgot you were here.'

Jamie kept staring.

'I was praying,' John explained. 'I was talking with God. I do this every night.'

'Like this?' Jamie whispered. 'You talk to God as if you knew him. As if you knew him very well.'

John started to answer, but Jamie slid back down and all but disappeared into the soft feather bed. He was already back to sleep again.

TIME TO MOVE ON

Nothing more was said about it the next morning; it was John's horses that Jamie had on his mind.

'I've never seen such beautiful horses,' Jamie said at breakfast the next morning. 'Hackneys!'

'Ah yes,' John said. 'They're beautiful fillies. My father gave them to me. Lassie and Lady, I've named them.'

'I'd like to take care of them for you,' Jamie said. 'They're very special horses.'

'That you may,' John said. 'And I'll be grateful to you. From this minute on, you're in charge of Lassie and Lady. They'll be your family.'

And so, before the week was out, John and Jamie became fast friends. They talked about horses and school and life. And they talked about God and prayer.

'I hear you praying at night,' Jamie said. 'I never heard anybody talk to God like that. You must know him very well.'

'Aye, I can never know him well enough,' John said. 'But you must learn to know him too – he's as close to you as your own hands and feet.'

When Sunday came around, the whole town of Selkirk seemed to awaken with a shudder. Cold! It was the kind of cold that bit your bones and made your nostrils stick together as if to shut out the freezing air.

The family drove to the rude little church in John's buggy. 'If I'm taking the new minister to church,' Mitchelhill chuckled, 'we might as well go in style.'

Lassie and Lady pranced along, lifting their hoofs high, tossing their heads, and snorting against the cold. Their breath came out in big puffs, sending billows of steam into the air. When they got to the church, John handed Jamie the reins as he climbed out of the buggy. 'Pull them around to the sheltered side,' he said. 'And put their blankets on so they'll be snug.'

'Yes, *sir*,' Jamie said, his face glowing with pride at being entrusted with so important a task. The rest stamped their way into the building. Some of the church officers had built a fire in a wood stove at one end of the big room. But a few feet away from it there seemed to be no heat at all; it was swallowed up in the bone-chilling cold that had been there all night.

In a few minutes people began to shuffle in. They sat on the rude wooden benches and wrapped themselves in shawls and blankets. Jamie came in too, and sat next to his parents. 'Pa,' he whispered, 'one of Mr Scot's servants is outside. He actually came to church!'

Mitchelhill raised his eyebrows in question. 'His handyman!' Jamie insisted.

'Aye,' Mitchelhill said. 'We'll have Scot himself here yet.' And he settled Jamie under part of his shawl and grinned across the room at John.

John nodded back, then looked over his new congregation from his pulpit. They stared at him expectantly. *What* they expected, he was not quite sure. For most of them seemed to be glowering. After they sang some psalms, he opened his Bible and began his sermon as if by the very fire of his preaching he would warm up the room. As he preached he looked at their faces.

'You're too young,' their eyes seemed to say, 'Dr Welch *indeed*!'

Mitchelhill was trying to look encouraging.

Mrs Mitchelhill looked glum.

And Jamie looked worried.

After the service, the people shuffled out solemnly, shaking John's hand at the door as if they'd been to a funeral. Jamie darted ahead of them, out into the cold. He was waiting by the horses when they got there.

'The blankets!' he cried. 'Somebody stole Lady and Lassie's blankets!' He exchanged glances with his father.

'It must have been Scot's doing,' Mitchelhill said, turning to John. 'His servant was here before church started.'

'I thought he was coming in to church!' Jamie said. 'I told Pa.'

John stooped and examined Lady's hoofs to see if they'd been injured. Jamie dived for Lassie's forefoot quickly, to do the same.

'They're all right,' John said at last, turning to Mitchelhill. Then, 'Let's get them moving,' he said to Jamie, 'It'll warm them up.'

'I should have known,' Jamie kept saying on the way home. 'I should have known he was up to something.'

'Don't blame yourself,' John said. 'It didn't hurt the horses. Mr Scot was being a nuisance.'

But he was uneasy. After Sunday dinner back home, he spoke to Mitchelhill about it. 'Why does Scot hate me so?' he asked.

'He doesn't hate *you*,' Mitchelhill said. "He hates *preachers*. Especially preachers who look prosperous. He just plain hates God. He's a wicked man."

'He's an unhappy man,' John said. 'And a foolish one, to be fighting God. I know. I spent years fighting God myself.'

'Aye,' said Mitchelhill. 'But don't worry. He's harmless. He was just weaned on a pickle.'

The rest of the winter was cold – but the cold in the air was nothing compared to the cold in most of the people's hearts.

As the weeks slid into months, the Mitchelhills and John settled down to being one big family. Mitchelhill was not quite right about the town. It wasn't bad, as he had said – it was worse, much worse. John met head-on with such hatred as he had never known before. 'The thieves on the border of England were jolly in comparison,' he told Mitchelhill as they sat by the fire one night. 'The older people hate me because I'm too young.'

'Well, lad, it's true you're young, and they

expected someone older,' Mitchelhill said. 'But they'll get used to you.' There was a comfortable silence. John was not angry, just puzzled.

'But the people my own age hate me because I preach against sin.'

'But so did Christ preach against sin,' the older man said with a twinkle in his eyes. 'Did you listen to *your* father, lad?'

John had to smile. 'No – I did *not*,' he said. 'I think, for a few years, I actually hated him. I just wanted to run away.'

'Well, then, you see, lad, that's how it is. And you know, some Scotsmen are jolly – and some Scotsmen are dour. And most of the Scotsmen in Selkirk are dour with a vengeance. Must be the cold winters. Wait till spring. They'll thaw out.'

'They look at me as if they'd been baptized in vinegar,' John said, but he smiled as he said it.

'Are you telling me you haven't got a mind to stay?' Mitchelhill said at last.

'I've had a call to go to Kirkcudbright,' John said. 'But I'll stay if God wants me to. I don't mind the hatred. I just want to be where God wants me.'

Mitchelhill got up slowly and banked the fire for the night. 'I have a feeling,' he said, 'that you're not afraid of danger. Or of hatred. I have a feeling that you're waiting for a sign from God. And when you get the sign to move on, you'll go with my blessing. And I'll be sorry to see you go.'

'I'd like to stay until God turns Selkirk upside down,' John said.

'Well, now, lad,' Mitchelhill said, 'maybe it's some other place God wants to use you to turn upside down. Who knows? He might have a mind to send you farther away than Kirkcudbright before he's through.'

As they parted for the night, neither of them realized just *how* far away John would go, or what unbelievable adventures he would have before his life was over.

'And don't mind Scot,' Mitchelhill called after

John. 'He's a wicked man, he is, but he can do you no real harm.'

John carried the letter from Kirkcudbright in his pocket after that and read it often. But he kept telling God, 'I won't budge from here unless you say so. Just cinch this letter with a sign and I'll be on my way.'

It wasn't until the following spring that God did.

* * *

Clearly, it was time to move on.

John accepted the call to Kirkcudbright.

Towns seem to have personalities, same as people do. About Selkirk, John had a feeling of great loss and a feeling of failure. If the personality of the ugly little town could be wrapped up in one word, it would be hatred.

He did not know it then, but he had left two people who would never forget him as long as they lived. One was Jamie, who'd listened to him praying at night.

The other was a young man named Ewart. Ewart was poor, but he did have two horses and a wagon. 'All I have to offer you, Mr Welch, is transportation to Kirkcudbright,' he said. 'For you know I'm a poor man.'

The Mitchelhills and Ewart helped John load up Ewart's wagon. They anchored John's buggy behind, and after sad farewells, John and Ewart were on their way.

As they started up the lane toward the road, John looked back and waved at the sad little family; the Mitchelhills looked as if they'd lost their best friend. The last person John saw was Jamie, running up the lane, struggling with his tears and waving wildly.

'God's blessing on you, Mr Ewart,' John said when they got to Kirkcudbright and unloaded the wagons at his new lodgings. And he handed Ewart a gold coin. 'Take it as a token,' he said. 'You will never want for money as long as you live.' He was not sure why he had said it; it had just come full-blown into his mind.

* * *

The feeling he had about Kirkcudbright was simply that he was not supposed to stay there very long. *But I like it here*, he thought. *I'm preaching the gospel and people are really listening.*

But that *feeling*.

It came to him in the most peculiar way. It was when he met Mr Robert Glendinning.

'Back from his travels,' the townfolk said excitedly. 'And what a grand gentleman he is.'

He was indeed. He was enough to dazzle the eye and send the senses swirling and make your silk socks roll up and down.

When John first saw him, the fine gentleman was dressed in scarlet silk and silver lace. John stopped in his tracks at what the Lord put in his mind to say. 'Mr Glendinning,' he found himself saying, 'you're going to have to change your fine silks and silver for more practical clothing.'

'What?' Glendinning's mouth dropped open.

'And stop buzzing around like a gadfly,' John went on. 'And start studying the Scriptures. For you're going to be my successor.'

What? Glendinning the next minister? This wastrel? This fop? *Why do I say things like this?* John thought. *How do I know things like this? Some of them seem so ridiculous that I sometimes think God has gone quite out of his mind.*

When word of this strange prediction got around, many people thought the good *Dr Welch* had gone quite out of *his* mind. Glendinning, a *minister*? All things were possible, of course, but Glendinning studying the Scriptures? Why Glendinning had not read anything but a dance program in years –

But wait a minute. While people were laughing, something astonishing was taking place.

Glendinning discarded his silks and lace; he soon had his nose in the Bible and his heart fixed on God. And by the time John was ready to leave Kirkcudbright and move on to his next post, Glendinning was ready to take his place!

John was headed for Ayr this time. *Tally ho*, he thought. *Straight ahead. This time for high adventure!*

If it was adventure he wanted, it was adventure he got – beyond his wildest dreams.

ELIZABETH SAYS YES

Ayr! It was a much bigger town than either Selkirk or Kirkcudbright.

John's feeling here was one of excitement. Which was strange, because the place was one of wickedness. Not the stiff and dour cruelty of the Christians in the other towns, but out-and-out rowdy knock-down-drag-'em-out wickedness!

At any rate, Selkirk and Kirkcudbright were in the past.

Selkirk, except for a few faithful followers and Jamie, had been a disaster.

And Kirkcudbright had gone by so quickly that it seemed to have passed in a flash. Indeed it seemed that he had stopped there only long enough to spin Glendinning around in his tracks so God could use him. And here he was at Ayr. It was the spring of 1590 and he had arrived a few days before, full of enthusiasm and raring to go.

This time he was living at the house of a gentleman named John Stuart, a one-time provost* of Ayr, and a Christian. John had part of the house for his own quarters.

Now he was wandering about the town with Mr Stuart – up one street and down another, looking in the shops, stopping to listen to gossip. This was going to be his town for a long time, he thought, so he might as well get acquainted with it.

Mr Stuart hadn't wanted him to venture out alone. For if there was one thing the people in the town loved to do, it was to fight. The day they did not have a good fight was a day wasted, they thought. Fighting was the town pastime – it was a way of life. A fellow could get into a scrap at the drop of a hat and without half trying. Mr Stuart had warned him. Just

---

* *The chief magistrate, a high official.*

crossing the street or walking past the wrong tavern could get a chap knocked silly –

Whoa, there, what was this?

A fight going on just up the street!

John stopped in his tracks. The shuffle of feet, the shouts and cursing of men, and yes, the whack-whack of clashing swords!

These men didn't fool around; they really fought!

'It looks as if my ministry is going to begin a little sooner than I thought,' John muttered. 'This isn't the way I planned it. But this is the way it's turning out.'

Before Mr Stuart could stop him, John leaped forward, right into the midst of the fray!

'Welch!' Mr Stuart screamed. 'Don't. Don't, I tell you. Are you crazy?'

But John was too busy to listen, and he didn't feel at all crazy. In fact, he never felt better in his life.

'*Gentlemen, gentlemen*!' he shouted. He gave one of them a quick chop right in the bend of his arm and knocked the sword out of his hand.

They all stopped aghast, looking at John the way you'd look at a horse if he suddenly started to talk.

No one had ever called them *gentlemen* before!

Their mouths gaped open, and the rest of them dropped their swords to their sides. There was a great silence as people stopped to watch, flattening themselves against the shops and taverns that lined the street.

Not one of them spoke. Not one of them could; they were stupified. Stuart stood a safe distance away, trembling in his boots.

'This is no way to settle a quarrel,' John said quietly. 'Even if you're right. What's the good of being right – if you're dead?'

'Welch?' Stuart stammered again. John turned around. But he didn't look at Stuart; he was looking at the open door of a tavern where a very plump proprietor was standing, his mouth gaping open.

John clapped his hands.

'Sir,' he called out. 'Would you bring out a table.'

'A *what*?'

'A table.'

'There in the street?'

'Yes, yes, and quickly. And bring a cloth too. We'll do this in style. We're going to eat and drink together – as soon as these fine gentlemen have made up.'

'You want food and drink too?' the proprietor cried in total disbelief.

'Yes – yes!'

Crazy!

But the craziest part of all was that everyone did as he was told!

The men stood still, as if they were playing a game of statues. Now the fight began to look like a comic opera.

Seconds later the proprietor came huffing and puffing out the tavern door with one of the kitchen boys, dragging a table. Then came the food. By now quite a crowd had gathered. This was a far more interesting spectacle than a fight would have been!

'Now, gentlemen,' said John, 'we must say grace.'

'Grace?' they muttered. 'Who's she?'

'I mean thank God for the food,' he said cheerfully. 'And remove your hats, gentlemen.'

Off came the hats – feathered hats, stocking caps – all of them. One man was so confused he started to remove a patch from his eye, then thought better of it and removed his stocking cap instead.

'Oh,' John said. 'And put your swords back in their sheaths. You won't need them – unless you want to use them to butter your bread.' They put their swords back and stood there, silent. He offered a brief prayer of thanks to God. Then he began to break off chunks of bread from a huge loaf, and pass them around.

Mr Stuart came over very slowly. He looked so bewildered it was almost comic. It was as if he didn't know whether they had called a minister or a madman.

'Now, gentlemen,' John said as he made room for Mr Stuart at the table. 'This is Mr. John Stuart, a very eminent official in town.

You're in good company.'

The men nodded, silent, and started to eat. There was very little conversation; it was as if they were mesmerized.

At last they were finished.

'Well, now, if you gentlemen will excuse us,' John said as he wiped his hands on his handkerchief. 'We'll be on our way. And I hope to see you all Sunday.'

Finally, one of them found his voice. 'Who *are* you?' he said.

'Oh, didn't I mention it?' John said innocently. 'I'm the new minister. My church is a little way out of town, but not too far for you to walk. Good-bye, gentlemen.' And he turned and walked away, with a still-bewildered Mr. Stuart trailing along.

As they passed the still-puffing proprietor, John opened his money bag, dumped out some coins, and put them in the proprietor's outstretched hand. 'Thank you, sir,' John said. 'This has been very nice; we should do this more often.' And then he walked away.

The people who had been watching stirred themselves. They, too, had been still, like children playing "statues." Now they began to move in slow motion.

'I can't believe it,' Mr Stuart said. 'It's as if you had some strange power over them, as if you had cast a spell.'

'I lived with a band of thieves when I was a young lad, much to my shame,' John said matter-of-factly. 'I know all their tricks. But power? Ah, the power – that is from God.'

At suppertime that evening they were still all talking about it. 'Which reminds me,' John said when the meal was finished, 'I'm going over to the church to be alone with God. I want to pray. I probably won't be back until morning.'

'You're going to pray all *night*?' They stared at him.

'Yes – yes, I probably shall. It will take me all night to thank God for what he did for me this afternoon.'

'But, Welch!' Stuart began. 'It isn't safe to walk these streets at night!'

'I'll be all right,' John said.

'Yes,' Stuart said, shaking his head in amazement. 'Somehow I think you will be.'

John started for the church. Indeed he did have a great deal to thank God for. He had a lot to tell him – and a lot to ask him. For now it was clear to him that he did have power – the power of the very Holy Spirit of God!

And he had a strange feeling of excitement about the city of Ayr. He knew, somehow, that he was going to be very powerful, that he was going to find a house of his own to live in – and that he was going to ask Elizabeth Knox to be his wife. And that God was going to grant his wish.

She would say yes.

He quickened his step; he could hardly wait to get to the church to talk it all over with God.

DARK DAYS TO COME

Elizabeth stirred in her sleep. The fires in the fireplaces had long since gone out, and the house was cold. It was early spring in Ayr in the year of 1602. It had been a long cold winter, and the frost was still upon the earth. Elizabeth stirred again and then opened her eyes. She was snuggled deep in the feather bed, covered with a huge down comforter pulled up to her chin. Her nose was cold, but the rest of her was snug and warm, so it was not the cold that had awakened her.

It was a voice. In the next room. She reached over to the other side of the bed. It was empty. By the way the moonlight shone across the room she judged it was about two in the morning. She struggled up from under the comforter and sat on the edge of the bed. Pulling on a woolly robe, she sank her feet into warm bed slippers.

'It's John again,' she sighed to herself. 'When does he ever sleep?'

Elizabeth was no longer Elizabeth Knox, she was Elizabeth Welch. For John had indeed asked her to marry him and she had said yes, just as God had told him she would. She had been married to John for twelve years now, and had borne him three fine sons. And they were living comfortably in a large house of their own.

At first she had been a bit frightened, for this new husband of hers was not tamed by marriage; in fact, he was more of a tiger than ever. He was forever rushing into the midst of sword fights, demanding tables to be set up in the middle of the street, making the fighters eat – and then inviting them to church!

One of these days, she kept telling herself in the first few months of their marriage, he'd get himself sliced up like a roast of mutton, and she'd be a widow before she'd hardly got a chance to settle down as a wife.

But none of this had happened. Instead the street fights had grown fewer and fewer until they had stopped altogether. The ruffians in the town finally decided that it was no use to start a fight, for Pastor Welch would soon be along to stop it. They had finally concluded that if you couldn't lick Pastor Welch, you might as well join him.

So they had all finally wound up in church!

Indeed, practically everyone in town listened to Dr Welch. They hardly made a decision without asking him first. For this man Elizabeth had married had a strange power about him.

She crossed the room, stopped at the door, and listened.

'Lord,' cried John, 'will you not grant me Scotland? Not just Ayr? But all of Scotland?'

Then there was a silence. She started to open the door; then she heard his voice again.

'Enough, Lord. Enough.'

She opened the door and stood framed in the doorway, her hair hanging down her back in one thick braid. John had been pacing the floor, but he stopped when he saw her. He opened his mouth to speak but she was one step ahead of him.

'Dr Welch!' she said. Elizabeth never called John "Dr Welch" except when she was being very stern. John, yes, and sometimes even Johnny, but never Dr Welch.

Now if there was one whom John held in awe above all others, it was God. But the only human being who could stop him in his tracks was Elizabeth. 'The fire is out,' she went on sternly.' And this room is not just chilly – it's cold. You'll catch your death!'

They stared at each other for a moment. 'Elizabeth,' he began sternly, 'what are you doing up at this hour?'

'What do you mean?' she went on, ignoring his question. 'Will God grant you all of Scotland? And what did you mean by "Enough, Lord. Enough"?'

'Elizabeth,' he said, clearing his throat, 'curiosity killed a cat.'

'I am not a cat,' she shot back. 'I am your wife. Elizabeth Knox Welch. Remember me?' She took a shawl from the sofa and wrapped it around his shoulders. 'And I'm concerned about your health.'

'I asked God for all the souls of Scotland,' he said sighing.

'What did you mean by "Enough, Lord. Enough"?'

'He promised me a remnant. Only a few. I am grateful for this. But Elizabeth –' he took her by the shoulders, 'there will be dark days ahead – very dark days.'

'What's going to happen?' she asked. 'Did God tell you?'

'No,' he said. 'We must just trust him. If I knew all the details there'd be no room for faith.' His voice was stern but his look was tender. He was as much in love with Elizabeth as he'd been back in Edinburgh. She turned and started for the door.

Elizabeth was a woman of great spirit and when it came to an argument she was no slouch. But she was also smart enough to know when to quit. She turned at the door. 'Whatever sad days are ahead,' she said, 'I'm ready for them. No matter how bad they are.'

Neither of them could possibly know just how bad those days were going to be.

* * *

It was only a matter of weeks when trouble struck. Like some giant monster that had been asleep for many years, a deadly disease awoke and stretched and yawned. It came stalking across the land.

The plague! It ravished the countryside and it spread like wildfire, from one person to another, from one family to another – from one city to another.

There were "clean" cities and "plague" cities. Every city guarded its ports and entrances.

Ayr, so far, was a "clean" city.

John went on with his ministry and

Elizabeth went on with her duties at home, bringing up their three sons.

And then one night the plague knocked at the doors of Ayr.

They did not know it – even John did not know it. It began with a knock on their door. They were eating supper. 'Dr Welch,' the messenger said, 'there are two merchants outside the city, at the west gate. They beg for permission to come into Ayr and sell their wares.'

'And?' John said, rising from the table.

'Well, they have a certificate from the town they just left. It's clean. We were going to let them in but we thought we'd better ask you first.'

'I'll be right there,' John said. He left his supper and hurried after them, through the narrow cobblestone streets, to the gate. And there, sure enough, were two healthy-looking merchants. And horses with packs of merchandise on their backs.

'Do we let them in?' the guards asked.

John examined their certificates. It was true; they had come from a clean town. By all the laws of common sense they should have been let in. But John said, 'Wait.'

He walked over to their horses and raised his face to God. He stood for such a long time in silence that the men around him began to shuffle their feet with impatience. Then John finally turned back to them. 'I cannot let you in,' he said.

'But we're clean!' they cried. 'You saw the certificates. We're clean.'

'But the plague,' he said softly, 'is in the packs on your horses. We cannot let you in here. I beg you not to go on, to bury your packs; you will only spread death.'

But they did go on, and in a huff. As they rode off, John cried after them, 'I beg you. The plague is in your packs!'

'But they had certificates from a clean town,' Elizabeth said when John got back home. 'How did you know?'

'God showed me,' he said simply. 'And I

begged them to bury the packs. God help the next town they go to. God *help* them.'

* * *

Elizabeth's hair was escaping in little tendrils down her neck. She had worked all day in the kitchen with the cook. The Welches were having a large gathering of friends in for the evening. There was food aplenty, and, so far, Ayr was still clean.

When the guests arrived, Elizabeth was dressed in her best, and so were the boys, their hair slicked down. Even their necks were clean – "cleaner than they've ever been before," the boys informed their mother.

The gaity continued far into the evening; the house rang with laughter and song. It was not until a lull in the singing that they realized John had not been with them for some time.

'Where is Dr Welch?' someone asked.

Where, indeed, *was* the minister?

'He's out in the garden,' Elizabeth said. 'Probably talking with God. He'll be back.'

But he didn't come back.

And he *didn't* come back.

Two hours went by.

Now, of course, these people all prayed, but never in their wildest dreams had they imagined that anyone prayed for as long as John Welch did. They'd heard about it, but it was hard to believe.

A few of them went to the window to look. 'What's he doing?' someone whispered.

'He's just walking in the garden,' the report came back. 'But there's something very strange – there's a light around him – I've never seen anything like it.'

They all hurried to the window to look.

'It's all around him!' someone cried. 'The most unearthly mysterious light!'

They all watched in silence. 'Just leave him alone,' Elizabeth said. 'He's talking with God.'

It was then that the messengers knocked on the front door. It was a report from the town of Cumnock where the merchants had gone.

It was filled with the plague.

There were hardly enough left alive to bury the dead.

The plague, sure enough, had been in the merchants' packs!

'We must tell Dr Welch!' the guests cried, and one man started for the door to the garden.

'No,' Elizabeth said. 'Don't disturb him. I think he probably already knows. I think what we must do now is stay in here and pray for that unfortunate town.'

And they did. And what started out to be a party ended as a prayer meeting.

'Are these the dark days you prophesied?' Elizabeth said later, when they were in bed.

He reached over and grasped her hand. 'No, Elizabeth,' he said. 'These are not the dark days. The real dark days are yet to come.'

'And what are they?'

'I don't know, Elizabeth. God has not told me. But there are dark days ahead. And we had better be ready for them.'

They finally fell asleep.

There were dark days ahead indeed – dark days that would have far-reaching effects on all their lives.

The dark days began in 1604. Trouble had been simmering like a pot of porridge on the back of the stove for years, but now –

'It's not simmering now,' John told Elizabeth. 'It's boiling. There are rumours that the king is planning to abolish the Assemblies of the Protestant ministers.'

'But he was brought up a Protestant,' Elizabeth said. 'My own father preached at the king's coronation when his Catholic mother* was forced off the throne. King James the Sixth. He was scarcely more than a year old – an adorable little child.'

'He had one problem,' John said dryly. 'He grew up.'

'John!' Elizabeth looked at her husband sternly.

'Now he's neither fish nor fowl,' John went on, ignoring her. 'He has only one goal in mind – the absolute authority and divine right of the *king*. He's thinking only of his own power. The Protestants are too independent for him –'

'John, he *is* the king –'

---

* *Mary, Queen of Scots*

'Too independent for him,' John repeated. 'And he intends to rule through his Catholic bishops.'

'But he never bothered us before,' Elizabeth said, and then she was silent. She remembered the stories of how her own fiery father had battled his way through years of Mary's fierce opposition.

Had the darling little child at whose coronation Knox had preached, grown up to be a tyrant? They were soon to find out.

* * *

King James VI sat on his throne and shouted at his advisors. 'My bishops will be head of the church!' he bellowed. 'These Protestant rebels are planning to meet in their General Assembly and proclaim Christ head of the church.'

'What do you propose to do, Sire?' they asked.

'I propose to destroy the General Assemblies. As long as they can meet together in freedom *I* am no longer the head of the church, nor are my *bishops*.'

'But you can't just cancel the General Assembly. You gave them permission to hold it two years ago. That would make you a tyrant; the whole country would be in an uproar,' his advisors said.

'No,' said the crafty king. 'They have appointed their next meeting to be in Aberdeen on the last Tuesday of July, 1604. I shall simply postpone it.'

He put his fingers together like a steeple and pursed his lips. Somebody began scribbling. 'By my orders,' he began, 'the next meeting will be postponed until the first Tuesday of July – 1605.'

And that did it. The year went by. It was June, 1605 – a month before the postponed meeting was to take place. Then King James struck another blow. 'I hearby declare that this Assembly is absolutely prohibited – and this time it will not be postponed.'

The news spread abroad over the land.

The king had won the cold war.

* * *

'Elizabeth!' John said, bursting into the house one evening. 'Elizabeth, have you heard the news? The king has prohibited the General Assembly in Aberdeen.'

'What are you going to do?' Elizabeth asked.

'I'm going to Aberdeen, of course,' he said matter-of-factly.

'John!' she cried, terrified. 'You'll be arrested. You may be thrown in prison. Or even killed!'

'I'm going to Aberdeen,' he said firmly. 'The Christian ministers throughout the country have still purposed to go to Aberdeen. They'll just meet, bring the meeting to order, then adjourn it – and dissolve. Just to show the country that we're still alive and kicking.'

Elizabeth signed; she knew better than to argue.

'I'll be gone for a few days,' John said that night at supper. 'I'm going to Aberdeen. Even if we can't hold the meeting, we can meet and adjourn.'

'To face the king's wrath?' his sons asked.

'To face the king's wrath.'

'But isn't that dangerous?'

'Oh yes, very. But I'm not going alone. God is going with me.' He looked at Elizabeth. 'I must,' he said.

'Then the days of the plague – those weren't the dark days?'

'No, Elizabeth, those were only the beginning. The real dark days are still to come.'

* * *

John Welch walked down the main street of Aberdeen. The Assembly was over; he had not arrived in time. He was on his way to look up some friends when a heavy hand fell on his shoulder. 'You are Dr. Welch?' a voice said. It was one of the king's officers.

'Yes,' John said. 'I am. What do you want?'

'You were at the convention?'

Well, now, right there, John could have wriggled out of it. All he had to do was to tell them he was not at the convention, which would have been the truth.

'No, I was not,' he said. Safe so far.

Then he went on. 'But I am in total sympathy with it. The king has no right to say that he and his bishops are the head of the church. *Christ* is the head of the church and that's what this Assembly is all about. And had I arrived in time I would have been there with them.'

Well, that stopped them short. Who was this madman who could have simply told them he was not there, and been let off scot-free. Was he crazy?

They let him go for the time being, for they had no orders to arrest him. But they muttered as they watched him go on down the street. 'That minister,' they said, 'is out of his mind. Doesn't he know that he does not have a prayer?'

John knew, as he walked away, that he was a marked man, all right. But he also knew that he was *not* out of his mind. And that he *did* have a prayer.

When he got back to Ayr, he told his family

about what happened in Aberdeen. They all prayed about it and committed him to God's care.

But a feeling of uncertainty was in the air; something was going to happen, of that they were sure – but *what*?

As the days rolled into weeks, however, it began to look as if the answer was – *nothing*. Things went on without a sign of trouble; it looked as if the peevish king had quite forgotten his tantrum. The talk around the table grew jolly again. And Elizabeth even got back to taking John to task about his health.

'Dr *Welch*!' she scolded one night as she rushed out to the garden, pulling her robe about her. She scolded in a stage whisper that could have been heard a block away. He knew she was furious. He stopped pacing, but he kept his back to her.

'Dr *Welch*?' she scolded again. 'Do you realize that it is nearly four o'clock in the morning – and that it is chilly and damp out here? Isn't it dangerous enough that you never get your proper sleep? Do you have to get a chill, too? Come inside – please!' She said it all in one breath; indeed it looked as if John was in for a nonstop scolding.

'Come inside this instant,' she went on, 'I implore you to think of your –'

That's as far as she got.

He turned slowly to face her. He looked pale and drawn in the moonlight, but his eyes were glowing with a strange light.

It stopped her short.

'Elizabeth,' he said quietly, 'I shall never preach at Ayr again.'

'What do you mean?' She tried to sound stern, but her voice was shaky. 'You're preaching next Sunday.'

He shook his head. 'I'll never preach here again, Elizabeth. I preached my final sermon in Ayr last Sunday. God is sending us away.'

'Where? What do you mean?'

'I don't know where. God hasn't told me. I only know that I'll never preach here again.'

They went back to the house slowly,

without speaking – an air of mystery surrounding them. They were like two children groping for answers, and there were none.

John was right. Within the week he was arrested and dragged off to prison.

Dragged off to prison merely because he was in sympathy with the Protestants.

The days ahead looked dark indeed. Even the name of the prison was – *Blackness*.

From there he went to trial for high treason. And the sentence was worse than anything John or Elizabeth could have dreamed.

Banishment from Scotland forever – never to return again.

BANISHED

It was getting along toward winter now. The wind was cold. It bit into them as they huddled together on the beach, waiting to be deported to France, by order of the king. They were like shadows in the darkness, John and his little family, and a group of friends who had come to see them off.

Everything that could be said had been said, and now they sat on the hard ground, silent in their grief, waiting for the ship to sail.

One of them got up and moved over to where John was and squatted before him. 'Remember me?' he said. 'I'm Ewart. I'm the chap who moved you from Selkirk to Kirkcudbright, remember?'

'Ah, yes!' John's eyes lighted up. 'You transported me when they cut the rumps off my horses and left them to die. I remember well. And how does it go with you?'

'Remember you gave me a gold coin and told me that I would never want again?'

'Yes, I remember.'

'It has gone well with me; I have prospered ever since. I'm well off now.'

'And you came down here from Selkirk to see us off?'

'Yes. And to pray with you. And to offer you any help I can. Do you need money?'

'I need nothing,' John said, 'but the grace of God. I'm glad my prophecy came true. And glad you came. May you prosper forever. And you will.'

At that moment the shout went through the night – 'All aboard!'

The guards in charge began to separate the prisoners from their friends.

They all rose stiffly from their sitting and kneeling positions. They had prayed all night for this hour; it was about three in the morning. And now it was time for John and Elizabeth and their children to leave for France. They sang the twenty-third Psalm; then there were hugs and tears as they all bade each other good-bye. John and his family were hustled up the gangplank and on to the ship.

Then the ship pulled up anchor and they were on their way.

* * *

Banished from Scotland. And to where? To France, a land of complete confusion and chaos.

The nobles were against the monarchy.

The middle class was against the nobles.

The Catholics were against the Protestants.

The Protestants were against the Catholics *and* the monarchy.

'But what will you do in a strange country?' John's friends had cried, and he had answered, 'I may be exiled from Scotland but I'm a long way from being stopped.'

'But what will you do with the language?'

'I'll learn it,' he said.

What? Preach in French? That would be enough to stop any ordinary preacher.

But John was no ordinary preacher. He was unstoppable.

Behind him forever was his familiar and beloved Scotland.

Ahead of him was France and the unknown.

Adventures beyond anything he had ever dreamed.

LANGUAGE LESSONS

St Jean d'Angely was a town of considerable size. It had great walls around it and was perched in the midst of the most beautiful countryside of France, with rolling hills and farmlands surrounding it. And guess who was preaching there?

John Welch!

John Welch preaching in French? Yes, John Welch preaching in French. For when they had asked (like prophets of doom) what he would do with a strange language, he had replied matter-of-factly, "I'll learn it".

And he had set about to do just that. He and Elizabeth had settled in with their little family in a large house. And while Elizabeth cooked and watched over the children, John stayed in his study and wrestled with French.

He studied. And studied. And studied.

The weeks went by. Two weeks. Three weeks. And then a month.

And John struggled with his verbs and syntax and sentence structure and all the horrifying things that go along with learning a language.

Now you might say it would be reasonable enough if he had learned to speak French well in a year. Or, better still, in six months. But John Welch learned to speak French – *in fourteen weeks*!

In fourteen weeks he was not only speaking French, but he had been called to a church. And he marched up to his new pulpit, and *preached*.

Of course, at first he read his sermons. But this was very difficult for him to do. His heart was so on fire for God, he simply could not stick to just reading the words on paper. When he'd get a sudden thought he would wander away from the familiar words, and his French would become so garbled that he would say one thing while he meant another. And sometimes his sermons would turn into a circus and he would catch the smiles all over his new congregation.

He murdered verbs.

He slaughtered nouns.

He misplaced words.

He tore up sentences in little pieces and sent them flying into the air.

'Welch,' his elders told him, trying to keep from laughing, 'you must stick to your written text and not get carried away with such passion. When you get carried away, you carry our language away with you.'

'I cannot read a sermon,' he shot back. 'My heart is too full. I have to empty what is in my heart.'

They looked at him sadly, but smiling too, for some of the things he said were quite ridiculous.

'All right,' he said at last, 'there must be

some way to solve this. I'll tell you what we'll do. You pick out several men who will understand what we're trying to do and who are willing to help me. Place them in different parts of the congregation – some in the back, some in the middle, some in the front. And when my heart waxes hot and I start scrambling the language, let one of them stand up, and I'll know I've gone awry.'

They smiled and bowed, eager to do his bidding, they loved him so.

'After all,' he said with a twinkle, 'when I'm trying to say, "*This is a day the Lord hath made; let us rejoice and be glad in it,*" I don't want to wind up saying "My grandfather's umbrella is on the hall table".'

They roared with laughter. So everyone took it good-naturedly. The whole congregation understood the problem and went along with it in deepest sympathy. And sometimes with great laughter and joy, too, for some of the mistakes he made were enough to stand your hair on end.

The result was that Dr Welch had one of the happiest congregations in the whole of France. They came to delight in his mistakes, to hear him murder their language, yes. But most of all they came to hear this great Scotsman with the warm and passionate heart and the unstoppable and unsinkable spirit. And in the midst of their laughter were tears. They warmed their hearts at the fire of God's great love for them.

And so in the end it was the same as it had been back in Ayr, in his beloved Scotland. Everyone loved him. They hung on his every word. And they stood in awe of the great gifts God had given him. He had answers to prayer such as they had not believed possible before.

He was lovable, fun, witty, and full of life. But most of all he had the warmth and charm of one who lives very close to God.

And so as the months went by, the men who were positioned all over the church to correct him stood up less and less as his mistakes got fewer and fewer – and finally not at all. He could preach circles around any other man in France!

Now all this was pretty difficult for Elizabeth and the children, for John practiced his French at home and insisted that it be spoken there as much as possible. And, of course, the children had to master it too, or they could not get along with the children at school, much less please their teachers and get their lessons done. They struggled with it good-naturedly, partly to please their father and partly to save themselves from embarrassment. After all, if you meant to say, "Father, may I have some of next week's allowance?" and said instead, "The eggs I gathered this morning are resting in the bathtub," you were out of luck. If you wanted your allowance, you'd better say it right.

After a while it was a hilarious game. They would often wind up in helpless laughter at the supper table. So, as the months rolled by, slowly but surely, they became a French family – a very happy French family.

By this time John's French was so excellent, and his preaching so powerful, that not only his own congregation listened to him, but he was invited out everywhere.

'Dr Welch!' said a wealthy member of his congregation once. 'I heard you preach at the University of Saumur last Wednesday.'

'Yes?' said John. 'You were there?'

'I was there,' the gentleman said. 'I was absolutely amazed. You spoke with such power and such authority.'

'Well?'

'But they were strangers. They were people of such quality and importance. How could you be so confident preaching to strangers like that?'

John paused a minute, and then chuckled. 'You are probably thinking of my French,' he said. 'Sir, I pulled my horses to a halt one day on the brow of a hill that overlooked a town in Scotland, where I'd been called to preach. It was a rough town, full of hate. No one there loved me or wanted me. I would never have survived if it hadn't been for God. And I've never forgotten it. Ever since then, when I'm going into a place where I might be afraid, I read his words again. And they lift me up soaring into the air like a kite. I am so filled with the power and greatness of God that there's no room left for me to be afraid of people.'

'Amazing, Dr Welch, amazing.'

'No, not amazing,' John said. 'For the Bible tells us that if God is for us, then who can be against us? If you believe this you have to live by it. It just makes good sense. It's that simple.' And with John it *was* that simple. This great and powerful man was really no mystery at all.

* * *

As the months rolled into years, France was slowly changing. King Henry IV died, and his young son, Louis XIII, was named the new king of France. His mother ruled for him until he was old enough to become the acting king. Unfortunately for France, he was a sickly boy, and not known for his brilliance.

The fact remained, however, that he was still the *king*. He may not have had the brain of a genius but he still had the power of a monarch, and his Prime Minister intended to keep it that way. And to keep it that way meant to keep the Protestants from having too much power, either political or religious.

John and his family were changing too. His family was growing. He didn't have any more children, but his house was bursting with boarders. There were students who came from all over France to board at his house and sit at his table and learn from him.

Elizabeth and the children sat by and listened too, for by now there were servants and cooks – and the dining room table got bigger as they kept adding to it, until it groaned with good food, nearly sinking in the middle like a sway-back horse.

There was learning, but there was laughter too, and prayers, and joy. It was the happiest big houseful in France, bursting with the love of God.

Now, of course, there are ups and downs in the happiest of lives, so naturally everything wasn't an "up."

One of the "downs" started with a simple headache. It belonged to a student, the son of a wealthy nobleman. And it grew worse at an alarming rate.

One night at supper, Elizabeth laid her hand against his forehead. 'He has a high fever,' she said. 'We must get him to bed.'

The young student pushed back his chair and tried to rise. 'I'll be all right,' he started, but that's as far as he got. He sank back in his chair, half fainting. It was plain that he was very ill.

Elizabeth called a servant and they led him off to bed. John and the students began to pray for him.

The days that followed were very solemn. The doctors were called, and Elizabeth nursed him, but he grew steadily worse.

Then one night, after teaching and prayers, John tumbled wearily into bed, confident that

Elizabeth would soon follow. The next thing he knew, Elizabeth was tugging at his arm. 'John,' she said, 'come quickly.'

He scrambled to his feet.

'We bathed him in cold water,' she said as they hurried toward the student's room. 'We've done everything we could for him.'

'We'll send for the doctor.'

She stopped him at the door. 'John,' she said softly, 'it's too late for a doctor. John – he's dead.' She opened the door and John went in.

The young man was, indeed, dead. His face was no longer flushed; it was pale now. John looked at him a moment, his heart bursting with love and anguish. This lad, so young, so full of promise! 'He can't be dead,' John said. 'He can't be.' And he raised his face toward heaven and began to pray. Just like the prophet Elijah had prayed for a dead lad in the Bible!*

* *1 Kings 17:19-23*

HE CAN'T BE DEAD!

When daylight came, a messenger was sent to the doctors, and to the student's family. By noon the house was abuzz with people. His grieving family had arrived with a coffin. They took him out of bed and laid him on a pallet on the floor so they could get him ready for burial. The doctors had indeed pronounced the lad dead. Everyone knew it; everyone but John.

'Leave me alone with him,' he said. 'I don't think he's dead.'

They looked at him in disbelief, but they closed the door and left him inside.

As the afternoon wore on, the door to the bedroom remained closed, John inside with the lad. Elizabeth whispered orders to the servants and made arrangements for his family to stay for the night. The cool evening breezes came in through the open windows. Elizabeth had an excellent meal served; they ate in silence.

'Please do as he said,' she told them. 'Go to sleep, get your rest. Tomorrow, we'll see.'

'I've sent for the best doctors in France,' the lad's father said. 'They'll be here in the morning. After that – no more waiting.'

The next morning the doctors came. John stepped aside as they went about their business. Was the young man dead? Who was right?

The doctors set about to find out. They pinched him with pinchers in the fleshy parts of his legs. They tied a bow-string around his head and tightened it. They did not have instruments in those days to tell if your heart and brain were still jumping. If they wanted to find out if you were dead, they *pinched* you. They worked by "guess".

'The weather is hot,' the family argued with John. 'We must get him into the coffin and bury him.'

But John insisted on having his way.

The day passed in silence. The meals went on as usual. The night passed in silence. John still remained in the lad's room. The next morning was solemn; everyone was angry with John. 'He is dead,' the doctors insisted. 'There is no more delay to be made. He must be buried at once. The weather is hot.'

John stood at the bedroom door, his hands outstretched.

'Please,' he said. "Please. I beg you once more. Leave me alone with him."

'Not another day!' everyone cried at once.

'Not another day,' John said. 'Just an hour. Give me an hour with him. I *beg* you. Just one more hour. What can it matter – just one more hour?'

They looked at each other in dismay. Then they shrugged and turned away in exasperation.

John closed the door.

One more hour.

He had been praying constantly. What could he not do? *I know he is not dead*, he thought, *I just know*. He fell to his knees, then stretched himself alongside the lad. He cried in his mind with all his might. 'God, I feel that this lad is not dead. I feel it in my very bones. God, help me. Don't let them bury this lad!'

He stayed there beside the student's body. 'If I thought he were dead I'd have given him up to you, Lord,' he muttered aloud. 'But I feel he is yet alive. Answer me, answer me, and let them know in this house that you are God –'

All of a sudden the student stirred. His eyes fluttered open. 'Dr Welch,' he said.

John nearly collapsed with relief and exhaustion. He got up on his elbows. He just stared at the young man; he could not speak at first. Then – 'Thank God,' he said, and then over and over again, 'Thank God ...thank God...'

'Oh,' the student groaned. 'My legs – my head.'

'It was the doctors,' John said. 'They put a bow-string around your head and tightened it. And they pinched you with pincers.'

He got to a sitting position and began to stroke the lad's head. 'You are very much alive,' he said. 'And your family is here.'

There was a soft tap at the door. 'Come in,' John said.

It was Elizabeth. She stood there, mouth open.

But before she could speak, he said, 'Yes, he's alive, Elizabeth. Somehow I knew it. Ask the cook to give you some broth for him. And then tell his family.'

She left, her mouth still open.

The rejoicing was a mixture of amazement and unbelief. The coffin was hauled back outside.

'It's just like the story of Elijah!' everyone cried. 'You brought him back to life!'

'Whatever happened,' John said, 'remember, God did it.'

The evening meal was not a jolly one with laughter, but it was indeed a joyous one. The lad was lifted back to bed, wobbly, but very much alive.

'You're wonderful,' everyone kept insisting.

'No – no,' John said. 'I simply felt that he wasn't dead. Whether or not he was, doesn't matter. I felt that he *wasn't*.'

'But we might have buried him!' they cried in horror.

'No,' he said. 'I would never have let you bury him. I'm a very stubborn Scotsman, as you must have seen by now.'

They all agreed. He was indeed a very stubborn Scotsman. He was also a man of miracles; by this time they knew it.

And as the story spread, nearly all of France knew it. This strange preacher was certainly a man to reckon with. People came to his door from all over France.

Like a certain Catholic friar who was travelling through the country, and happened on the Welchs house; whereupon he ran into John and got the surprise of his life!

SECRET VOICES

The friar was a monk in the Order of St Francis. He was travelling about the country, and came to the walled city of Jean d'Angely. He was hot and tired, and he wanted lodging for the night. The inns were all filled; he could find nothing. So he began inquiring.

'Do you know where I can find lodgings elsewhere?' he asked the innkeepers. 'In a private home, perhaps? I must get some sleep tonight.'

He didn't have to ask too long; Dr Welch's name was a household word.

'Dr Welch, of course,' they told him. 'You can always get lodgings there. He's a very tender-hearted man. He'll take you in.' They were safe in saying so, for Dr Welch, they knew, would take anybody in – even a Catholic friar.

So the good man got directions and found his way to John's door, and knocked. He was invited in with warmth. A servant called Elizabeth, and she came into the living room at once. 'Sit down,' she said. 'I'll tell Dr Welch. I'm sure he'll be glad to have you here.' The friar sank his ample frame into a comfortable chair and settled back gratefully.

Elizabeth went upstairs and came back after a few minutes. 'We've already eaten,' she said, 'and Dr Welch has retired for the night. But he is eager to have you stay; you are very welcome, and he wants you to be his guest.'

He started up from the chair.

'You have not eaten?' Elizabeth said.

He shook his head no.

'Then the servants will take your supper up to you,' she said smiling. She gestured to a servant, who took him up to his room.

There was a basin and a pitcher full of water

to wash with, and he got to work. While he was still splashing, there was a knock on the door, and a servant came in with a tray. He looked at it with delight; food was his pastime and his hobby. There were huge slabs of mutton, and vegetables and herbs and cheese and a flask of cold water. He muttered his thanks and tucked his napkin under his chin and settled down to eat. So, Dr Welch was a Protestant minister. No matter, this was a good house, better than any inn, he thought.

Later, he rummaged in his duffel bag for his nightshirt and soon climbed into the huge feather bed. There he heaved a big sigh of contentment and settled down for a good night's sleep.

* * *

A clock, somewhere in the house, struck two. The friar stirred in his sleep, then got up on one elbow, startled. It was not the clock that awakened him. He cocked his head and listened. It was something else.

A voice. A voice in the very next room. First

the voice. Then silence. Somebody was talking to somebody *who wasn't there*!

Now the good friar was bolt upright in bed. After all, he thought, he was lodging in the house of this strange Scottish minister. Perhaps the house was haunted. Or perhaps the voice was the voice of the minister himself. But whoever he was talking to was not talking back.

Could it be – could it be – the friar's hair stood up at the thought – that the minister was talking to – was talking to – the devil himself! That was it. He is talking to the *devil*. He *must* be talking to the devil! Horrors!

He was trapped in a houseful of devils. The poor friar sank back in his pillows, his teeth rattling, and pulled the covers up over his head. After awhile, exhaustion took over, and he drifted off into fitful sleep.

* * *

The next morning he awoke with a start. He scrambled out of his nightshirt and into his habit. Then he hastily packed his duffel bag and went downstairs.

The family was already assembled at breakfast. Dr Welch was at the head of the table, and he was reading the Bible to his huge family of wife and children and students. The friar waited, silent.

When the minister had finished, he turned to the friar. 'I'm glad you're here,' Dr Welch said. 'I hope you had a good night's sleep.'

'Yes, oh yes, yes,' the friar said nervously, and he was politely seated, amidst introductions all around.

But then the children and the students began to ask the minister questions about what he had just been reading. And he explained to them, from the Word of God. Then they bowed their heads and prayed!

After that, breakfast was served, and the friar's love of food overcame his fears. He ate without saying a word, thinking the faster he got out of this house of devils the better it would be for him. He spoke only when spoken to, and then all he could find to say was, 'Oh yes, yes, yes, indeed.'

As soon as he was finished, he mopped his mouth with his napkin, pushed his chair back so quickly it almost tipped over, thanked them all, and bolted out the door.

Phew! He felt as if he'd escaped from something dreadful and threatening.

But *what*?

He hurried through the town, out the main gate, and into the countryside beyond. He walked past farmers' fields. He greeted the farm hands and they greeted him back.

'Good morning,' one of them said, coming up the edge of the road. 'How are you this morning?'

'I'm not quite sure,' said the friar, and sat down by the roadside, panting.

'And where did you lodge last night?' the farmer asked.

'At the minister's house, back in town – Dr Welch.'

'Ah, Dr Welch?' the farmer said. 'Good!'

'Good?' The friar stared at him in surprise. 'What do you mean, good? It was all *bad*.'

And then before the farmer could answer, he went on, blurting it all out – the voice in the night – all of it. 'I always thought devils haunted these Protestant ministers' houses. Now I *know*. There were devils in that house last night. I heard the minister talking to someone – who did not answer.'

'In the minister's house?'

'Yes, in the minister's house,' the friar said, and he was babbling by now. 'I do believe' – and he stopped to mop his brow – 'I do believe that it was the minister and the devil talking most of the night.' He stopped and mopped his brow again. 'Yes – yes. Most of the night. The minister and the devil. I'm convinced of it.' He stopped again for effect, expecting the farmer to be horrified too.

But the farmer was grinning. 'Ah no,' he said. 'What you heard was not the minister and the devil talking. You heard the minister talking to God.'

"Talking to *God*?" the friar sputtered.

'Talking to God,' the farmer went on matter-of-factly. "What you heard was Dr Welch at his night prayers.'

'You mean he was *praying*? All alone? Does the minister pray when he's *alone*?'

'Ah yes,' said the farmer. 'He prays – more than any man in France.'

How long the friar sat there, his mouth open, he did not afterward know. He only knew that when next he tried to speak, his throat was so dry he nearly choked on his tongue. Then he realized that the farmer was gone; he was alone.

* * *

It was late afternoon when the friar knocked again on the door of Dr Welch's big house. The good friar had been roaming the streets all day, waiting for evening to come, so he could go back to that strange house that had upset him so the night before.

He had to go back, he thought, to find out if the minister really talked to the devil; but that was with only one part of his mind. The other part of his mind could not dismiss the

words of the farmer: 'The minister prays –
more than any man in France.'

What kind of a man would pray half the
night? What would he find to pray *about*? And
did anyone – *could* anyone – really talk with
God like this? Just carry on a *conversation* with
him?

The friar jumped as if he'd been shot when
the door opened. He started to babble the
speech he'd prepared and rehearsed – that
he felt ill and quite unable to travel; could he
rest one more night before going on his
journeys?

But to his surprise he found he need not
have even prepared it, much less rehearse it;
he would have been welcome without any
explanation.

What a strange house!

He was delighted to find he was just in time
for supper. He did not want to miss supper.

Not because of the good food – and this
was strange, for food was his hobby – but
because he wanted to listen to the minister at

his table, to hear him talk with his family and his students about the Word of God.

He sat through dinner, quivering with excitement, and being very careful to say nothing but, 'Oh, yes, yes, yes, yes, yes.' That sort of talk could get you into no trouble.

He listened as the questions and answers flew back and forth; why, the minister made God so real. He seemed to be in the very room. Astonishing!

After supper the friar went eagerly to his bedroom, prepared himself for the night – and waited. And waited.

He did not blow out his candle, just sat, propped up in bed, waiting.

Then, about two in the morning – sure enough.

The voice in the next room began again!

He listened until he could stay in bed no longer. He jumped out as nimbly as his ample frame would allow, and sneaked out of his room and shuffled down the hall to the minister's door.

And stood there, listening.

Such conversation between man and God, he had never before heard, nor even dreamed. Why, he had always memorized written prayers and recited them like a schoolboy. His mind, by this time, was in such a jumble he thought he was going to explode. He sank to his knees outside the minister's door.

And listened. And listened. And then – he stopped short in his listening and realized two things at once. He was no longer afraid – all the fear had drained out of him. And in its place was a feeling he had never known before. It was a great *longing*, almost like a *hunger*, for this mysterious something that the strange minister had!

Hardly before he knew what he was doing, he had pushed the door open. It creaked at first, then swung wide – and the next moment John Welch and the Catholic friar were staring at each other in astonishment. John, astonished at seeing the friar in his nightshirt kneeling outside his door. And the friar astonished at what he had done!

The friar scrambled to his feet, as fast as his great weight would allow, and went toward the minister, with no idea of what he would say. Then the words tumbled out.

'I want to know God the way you know him,' he said earnestly. 'I want to be able to *talk* with him the way you do.'

John started to answer, but the friar rushed on, unable to stop, now that he had made the plunge. 'Last night when I was in bed I heard you talking with someone. I thought the house was spooked. I thought – I thought you were talking to the devil. But I talked to a farmer this morning and he told me – he told me that you prayed more than any man in France – that you were talking with *God*. So I came back – I had to know.'

He was weeping now, unashamed. 'I want to know God the way you do. I want to *know* him, more than anything else in the world.'

'You can,' John said. 'It's no secret, dear friar. You see, I joined a band of thieves once, when I was a lad. And then I decided to go back to my father. I went back to my human father, yes, but even more, I went back to my heavenly Father, and to Jesus. For Jesus *is* God – they are one and the same. I talked with him then, and I've been talking to him ever since. He has guided my life – every step of it – from that day to this.'

'But this *power* you have –' the friar gasped.

'This power is not my power,' John said. 'It is the power of God. And you can have it too.'

They prayed together then, and for the first time in his life, the friar really *talked* with God.

He was no longer the "poor friar."

He went back to his room a rich man.

The next morning he washed in his basin, but the water that washed over him was nothing compared to the peace that washed over his heart.

At breakfast, when John read the Bible and they prayed, the good friar joined in heartily. And after breakfast, he went on his way rejoicing.

Back at the house, John and Elizabeth were

rejoicing too. Life had had its "ups" and "downs" with them; this was most surely an "up."

* * *

But John knew in his heart that soon a "down" was coming – dark days were ahead again.

What they would be, he did not know, what they would hold, he did not know – he just knew they were coming.

But in all his life, he had never been prepared for *this*. It came like a thunderclap.

A DIRECT HIT

John's ministry had been very successful. He was *the* Protestant minister of the city of St Jean d'Angely. Everything was going well – too well. His fame had spread all over France.

It was only a matter of time before it reached the ears of the Catholic king – Louis XIII.

The messengers came with the news right after morning prayers. They were some of the town's top officials. John faced them in the living room and asked them to be seated.

'There is news – bad news, Dr Welch,' they said.

'I knew there was trouble coming,' John said. 'I just didn't know what it was. Tell me.'

'It's the king,' they said. 'The Protestant

influence in the town has been great – too
great. Word of it has reached the king.'

'And?'

'And he is furious.'

'He's going to forbid us to worship?'

'Worse than that, Dr Welch,' they said. 'It's
war.'

'Don't give up,' John kept insisting. 'Christ
is the head of the church; He will deliver us!'
And *then* came the night – a night none of
them would ever forget.

The day had been a quiet one.

'You've got to get some sleep, John,'
Elizabeth insisted early that evening.

'I can't,' he said. 'While the city is in such
danger – I can't.'

'But you are half dead from lack of sleep,'
she cried, her eyes flashing. 'The others are
watching in shifts. If you are not walking the
streets, you are upstairs praying – God *knows*
you must have sleep. What good will you be
to these people if you collapse from lack of
sleep?' And she put her hands firmly between

his shoulder blades and pushed him the stairs.

'All right,' he said at last. 'But you mu. wake me the moment anything happens.'

Everyone in town had made John the unofficial commander-in-chief, but this night, Elizabeth was the boss.

Up in his bedroom, she stood, her arms folded, until he had climbed into bed. He opened his mouth to scold her sternly and remind her who was the head of the house. But before he could get the words out, he was asleep. The last thing he heard was the click of the door being closed behind her as she went out of the bedroom.

* * *

Silence. The clock ticked on in the huge living room downstairs. And struck the hours. And then – suddenly – a blast!

It came out of the night from one of the king's great guns. A cannonball came roaring through the air, over the city walls, across the town, into the very house where John Welch was sleeping, through the window –

his very bedroom and –
the foot of his bed – nearly
!
with a snort, then started
sliding toward the centre.

He couldn't believe it. His bed was hit with
a cannonball – and he was still alive!

He crawled his way up to the edge of the
bed, scarcely knowing what had happened,
scrambled out to the floor, and started to pull
on his trousers.

There was a deathly silence. Then a
scurrying downstairs, and jumbled footsteps.

* * *

Downstairs they heard too. It seemed as if
the whole side of the house upstairs had been
blasted open. They rushed across the room,
getting stuck in the doorway, and scrambled
up the stairs to see Elizabeth running down
the hall toward them, wide-eyed, frantic. They
pounded on his door. 'Dr Welch!' they cried.
'Are you all right?'

'Of course. Yes, yes!' came the voice from

within. 'I'm getting into my clothes – I'll be out in a moment!'

'The cannonball went right through your bedroom.'

'Through my bedroom? It went right through my bed. Nearly split it from stem to stern. I must take a moment to thank God – you'll have to wait!'

'A cannonball split your bed – and you're thanking God!?!' they howled.

'Yes!' the voice came back. 'I'm thanking God that I wasn't sleeping in the *middle*.'

Well *that* was something. They waited in silence. After a few minutes, the door opened. And John Welch stood there, fully dressed – even to his hat!

'John!' Elizabeth cried. 'Are you really all right?'

'Of course I'm all right,' he said, but his voice was wobbly. He ploughed through the mob in the doorway and started down the stairs. 'What's wrong with our guns?' he shouted as he went. 'Aren't any of them working?'

'They're still working, we think, but we have no one to man them. No one has the courage – they all are terrified – they fled the wall in terror!'

'What?' he shot back. 'No one with courage to man them? With Christ on our side?' He plunged toward the front door to open it, found it already open, and nearly fell through it. He caught himself with great running steps and bolted down the street, the men after him.

Elizabeth closed the door behind them. The students and all the men who'd been in the house were gone.

The boys came back into the room, their eyes frightened, and gathered around her. 'Where's father?' they asked, trembling.

'He's gone out to man a gun,' she said, 'on the city wall.'

'But he'll be killed!' they wailed.

'He will not be killed,' she said. 'Your father is John Welch. My father was John Knox. Between them, we have more power in this house than this world dreams of.'

'But our gun is nothing against the king's,' they said. 'Our gun is...'

'And if I know your father – if I know your father – one gun is powerful enough to knock the king's gun into smithereens,' she said.

'But what can we do to help?' they wailed.

'The best thing would be to calm down then fight with them from here. We can pray.'

And they did.

* * *

Meanwhile John was racing headlong down through the streets, toward the city wall where one of the guns was positioned, the men following him. He got there to meet a group of bedraggled men, their faces blanched with terror.

'Is that gun up there still working?' he cried.

'Yes, it's working, but no one dares to go up and man it.'

'What do you mean, no one dares to go up there and man it?' he shouted. 'Where's the gunner?'

The man nodded, trembling.

'Then why aren't you up there manning the gun?'

'I can't go up there,' the man whimpered. 'I'm afraid.'

'You are *not* afraid,' John said, grabbing the man by the chest, pulling his clothes up in a bunch. 'And neither am I. Now get up there and man that gun.'

'Noooo,' the man moaned, his knees buckling. 'Besides, there's nobody to carry the powder.'

'What do you mean, nobody to carry the powder?' John said. 'I'll carry the powder. You're going up there, and I'm going with you – you hear?' And he lifted the man straight up and gave him a shove. 'Up with you!'

The man stumbled up the stone steps to the top of the wall, and hurried, crouching, toward the gun.

'Now,' John said, 'where's the powder bin?'

The man pointed, and John bent over and ran to the powder bin, scooped up a ladle full, and started back. 'Get ready!' he cried.

And then –

WOOSH!

A cannonball shot through the air straight for John. But it did not hit John; it hit *the ladle he was carrying* and knocked it right out of his hand.

It spun him around, and for a moment he didn't know where he was or what had happened.

The gunner was leaning against the gun, weeping with terror.

John stood stock-still for a moment, trying to get his bearings. Then he staggered back to the bin, whipped off his hat, scooped up some powder, and ran along the wall back to the gun. He wondered dimly why he'd ever put on his hat in the first place – he couldn't remember even thinking about it. But now he knew the reason.

'Ready!' he shouted. 'Pack it!'

The gunner worked like a robot, following orders; he was too frightened to think.

'Now aim it!' John ordered. 'Right toward that hill – and on the king's gun.'

The gunner did as he was told.

'Now *fire!*'

The cannonball shot through the air with a great *wooooosh!*

And then –

POW!!!

SPLAT!

The cannonball had hit its mark – the king's gun splattered in all directions.

It was totally destroyed!

'We got it!' John yelled from the wall.

There was a great roar from the street below.

The gunner sank to the ground with great shivering sobs.

John put his hands on the poor chap's shoulders. 'It's all right to be afraid. I've been afraid too – many times.' John helped him to his feet and led him back down the huge stone steps to the street.

The guns were silent.

The king's army had given up!

An hour later John staggered back into the

house, a group of men with him. Elizabeth and the boys met him with open arms. They led him to a chair, where he sank down, his knees wobbling; the after effect had set in.

* * *

When everyone had left and the boys had gone to bed, Elizabeth brought him a cup of tea and sat alone with him. 'You're a very brave man,' she said softly.

'Who is brave?' he answered. 'My knees threatened to buckle every step of the way. I was brave while I was doing it – but after it was over, I could hardly get my legs going to get back home.' He sighed, put his cup down. 'Elizabeth,' he said, 'you are married to a very frail, very human man.'

'I'm married to the most wonderful husband in the world,' she said.

'No,' he said. 'I'm married to the most wonderful wife in the world. The daughter of the great John Knox. Whatever have I done to deserve such an honour?'

'Well, you've done enough tonight,' she

said matter-of-factly. 'I have another bed all prepared for you. Get into it. And quickly. You need your sleep.'

He looked at her fondly. No nonsense about Elizabeth, he thought, and a good thing, too. For he would have put a lesser woman in her grave long ago.

Would the king finally give up the siege? John thought, later in bed. He was asleep before he could even guess at an answer.

A VISIT WITH THE KING

The news spread like wildfire all over the town the next day. The king's gun had made a direct hit on John Welch's house – right into his bed – while he was in it!

Incredible!

Early next morning the knocking began on his door. Streams of people from all over the city – anybody who was anybody called to see how Dr Welch was. And crowds of the curious gathered outside to gawk at the gaping hole in the upstairs wall where there had once been a window, and to see that Dr. Welch was indeed all in one piece.

But they had more than that to be thankful for. The siege was over. Yes, the king had decided to quit while *he* was all in one piece.

He sent some of his officials into the city to discuss the terms. And the terms were unbelievable. The citizens would have a right to all their civil liberties. They could live in peace. And they could "practice their religion". And the walls of the town would not be demolished.

That was good. There was only one little catch. The king wanted to enter the city with his court and visit there awhile.

That was *not* so good.

'It could be dangerous, Dr Welch,' the town bigwigs told him, shaking their heads gravely.

'Dangerous?' John said innocently, but his eyes were twinkling. 'What do you mean?'

'Yes, dangerous,' they said, exasperated. 'You know, Dr Welch, that the king will never allow a Protestant minister to preach in any area where he and his court are staying. What will you do?'

'Why, I'll preach,' John said. 'What else?'

'You'll be taking your life in your hands!' they cried. But they knew there was no sense in arguing further with this stubborn Scotsman.

'Are you really going to do it?' Elizabeth asked when they were alone, though she already knew the answer.

'Woman,' he said grinning, 'you sometimes ask the most foolish questions."

'You know, John,' she said laughing, 'sometimes I think you *enjoy* danger.'

'No, I *don't*,'he protested. He thought about it for a minute. 'But sometimes I *do* enjoy a good scrap. If it's for a good cause. And it does keep me on my toes.'

Elizabeth sighed, but she was not angry. She was secretly proud of her husband.

* * *

The king was as good as his word. He moved into town with his court and an uneasy truce began.

And John was as good as *his* word. The next Sunday he was in his pulpit, and preached with such fire that the very church seemed to tremble with the power of God.

But when the word got to the king. 'What?' he cried. 'Welch dared to preach? In the shadow of my court?'

'Yes, Sire,' his officials told him. 'And the people were not afraid to come out and hear him either. The church was *packed*!'

'The devil take him!' the king bellowed. 'If I get my hands on him I'll do more than split his bed in two. I'll split his *head* in two. I'll take him apart, piece by piece –'

'Sire, don't get yourself upset –' they begged. 'It would not be wise to harm this man now. He is the most loved man in the entire city.'

The king sat in silence for a moment, his face red, his eyes bulging. 'Let it be known throughout the city then that the king is displeased,' he said. '*Very* displeased. When he finds out just *how* displeased I am, I'll bet my whiskers that he won't dare preach next Sunday. If he does – if he does – I'll send one of my dukes and some guards with orders to haul him down from his pulpit right in the middle of his sermon, and drag him back here.'

The word spread throughout the city as the king hoped it would. And the question was on everybody's lips. Would Dr Welch dare to preach the following Sunday? Those who knew him by reputation speculated about it. Those who knew him well were sure he would.

By the time the next Sunday morning came, it was apparent to everyone that if anyone were to take the king seriously, the king would surely lose his whiskers.

When John and his family got up to the church, they stopped short in surprise. The crowds outside were unbelievable!

John's elders led him and his family around to a side door. And as they entered the church, a great hush fell over the huge crowd. Inside, it was packed to the doors. Everyone had been wondering if Dr Welch would really show up.

As John climbed the stairs to his pulpit, he looked cool and unconcerned – as if he hadn't the faintest idea what the fuss was all about. His elders descended some stairs to a room below, and got down on their knees to pray.

The service began with the singing of some psalms; then the great Dr. Welch got up to preach. There was such a feeling of expectancy in the air that you could almost cut it. And John preached with such fire it seemed as if the great church trembled beneath their feet. John had been as good as his word.

But so had the king.

Everything went splendidly until, right in the middle of John's sermon – it happened.

A bustle and a flurry at the back door of the church. Someone was coming in. Someone of great importance, for the people were stepping aside to let him pass.

Then he stood there in the doorway.

Everyone gasped as one person.

It was the Duke d'Espernon – followed by four of the king's guards!

The duke was dressed in satin brocade breeches and waistcoat, silk stockings, shoes with silver buckles – and lace at his throat and his sleeves. He swooped off his plumed hat and stood there, glaring. The guards looked like a cross between the Three Musketeers and Puss-in-Boots.

John knew, had known all week, that the rumours were true. The duke and the guards had been sent to haul him down from his pulpit.

They waited for him either to stop preaching or at least to falter.

He did neither.

'Ushers!' he called out, 'will you please give these gentlemen seats so they can sit down in comfort? They need to hear this!'

The effect of this was stunning. A shock went through the entire congregation. An earthquake could not have shaken them up any more.

Before they could recover, the ushers had pushed chairs behind the duke and his guards. Their knees buckled and they sat down suddenly, flabbergasted – and John went right on preaching without even breaking his rhythm or his stride – just as if nothing at all had happened.

A minute passed. Everyone waited. Another minute. Five minutes. Was it possible that the duke was not going to interrupt the doctor? Those who could see him sneaked cautious peeks at his face. How was he taking all this? Was he angry? Was he amused? Was he waiting for just the right moment to stand up and bellow something that would shoot John Welch right up out of his boots?

No – he was *listening*!

His face was serious and intent. He sat there rooted to his chair, mesmerized!

And John went on preaching and the duke went on listening and the people went on sneak-peeking, right through to the very end of the sermon, and through the closing song.

The last note of the psalm had hardly died away when the duke and his guards stood, then marched up the centre aisle. The church was silent as though it had been empty. All that could be heard was the sound of the footsteps of the duke and his guards. They reached the pulpit and looked up at John.

'The king wishes to see you,' the duke said.

'I shall go gladly,' said John. 'And at once.'
He nodded at Elizabeth, then came down the
stairs from his pulpit, and followed the duke
and the guards out of the church.

The people stepped back to make room
for them, and gawked silently. It was not until
the duke's carriages clattered away down the
street that they began babbling. They could
only guess what might happen; they would
have to wait and see.

*   *   *

The huge house where the king had quartered
himself and his court was like a mini-palace.
It was lavishly furnished – tapestries hanging
on the walls – great stone fireplaces – and the
richest of furniture.

John was ushered into a side room and
left with the guards. The duke went on into
the next room to speak with the king.

John didn't have to eavesdrop to hear their
conversation. There was no way he could *not*
hear it.

'You've been gone for *hours*. Why didn't you interrupt the minister? Why didn't you haul him down from his pulpit and drag him here to me as I asked you to? You've been gone long enough for him to have preached *two* sermons. What were you *doing*?' The king's words all came out in a rush.

'I was listening to his sermon, Sire,' the duke answered.

'What?'

'Sire, I have never heard any man speak the way this man did. He spoke with such power and such authority. I was *compelled* to listen. So I sat through his sermon and we waited until the last psalm was sung.'

'Then why didn't you bring him here afterward?'

'I did bring him here, Sire; he's waiting in the outer chamber.'

'Then what are you waiting for? Fetch him, fetch him!' The king was bellowing now in exasperation.

When John entered the room the king was sitting at the head of an enormous table. He was trying to look fierce, but instead looked more like a petulant child whose toy soldiers had just been taken away from him. He gave John what was meant to be a withering glance – and then dropped his jaw.

John had quietly dropped to his knees, and was talking to God silently, just his lips moving, asking him for wisdom.

The king was too surprised to interrupt.

The room was silent.

Then John got to his feet and stepped up to the king, looking dignified but respectful. There was an air of authority about him that made the king pause a moment before he spoke.

'How dare you preach in this city when I am here with my Catholic court?' he began in a low voice. 'Don't you know that it is against the laws of France that any minister should preach within the shadow of my court?' Now his voice rose in anger again. 'How dare you. And you had the Duke d'Espernon sitting there listening to you – a member of my own court. How *dare* you?'

'Sire,' John said, 'if you did right, you would come and hear me preach too.'

'Auuuuuuuugh!'

'Yes, and make all France hear me.'

'*Auuuuuuuugh*!!!'

'For,' John went on, 'I preach that you must be saved by the death and merits of Jesus Christ, and not your own. And I preach that, as you are the king of France, you are under authority to no man on earth.'

The king leaned forward and looked at John with astonishment. These were words he liked to hear. Under authority to *no man*, indeed!

'As the king of France, Sire,' John repeated, 'you are under authority to no man; only to the authority of God.'

He had the king's undivided attention now, so he hurried on. 'Those men you listen to put you under the authority of the pope of Rome. I would never do this. You are under authority to no one but Christ. No man is the head of the church, Sire – *Christ* is the head of the church.'

There was a silence in the big room.

'Well!' the king said at last, drumming his fingers on the table. Finding no further words, he drummed some more. 'Well, well.' More drumming. 'Well, well, well.' *More* drumming. And finally, 'Dr Welch, you shall be my minister.'

Well this was a bit *much*. John did not know what he had expected, but he had certainly not expected *this*.

'Yes – my minister,' the king said again, liking the idea better by the minute. 'You shall be the official minister of the *king*.'

John bowed respectfully, in silence, and waited to be dismissed. The king gestured to a guard. 'See that Dr Welch is taken safely back to his home,' he said.

Astonishing! A few moments later, John was being driven through the streets, toward home. It was one of the strangest Sundays he had ever spent. He had to chuckle as he wondered what Elizabeth would say to *this*.

* * *

Within a week, King Louis had left the city in peace, with his court. And things settled back to normal. The siege was over.

John had an uneasy feeling, though, and he could not seem to shake it off. There was trouble ahead; he felt it in his very bones.

Night after night he prayed long hours, asking God why he should feel so uneasy and what was going to happen. The only answer he could get was that there were dark days ahead.

The weeks went by, and the months. The gaping hole in John's upstairs bedroom had been repaired. He preached without any interference. It looked as though the king had decided to leave them in peace. But Louis XIII was a man of many moods. Would he repent of his decision to make peace with the Protestants of St Jean D'Angely? Would he change his mind? Something was going to happen. John knew – but *what*?

LET HIM PREACH HIS HEART OUT!

It was only a matter of months when trouble crashed down on them like a bolt of lightning and turned their lives upside down. Nothing was ever to be the same again. For King Louis did change his mind.

War!

And this time with a vengeance!

War!

The town officials were at John's door the moment the news came. "Dr Welch, do you have any word from God?" they said. "Will we be able to hold out against them this time?"

He did not speak for a long moment and they searched his face for an answer. It looked gray and drawn and very, very tired. He had been up all night in prayer. 'This time there will be no escape,' he said at last. 'This time the king will take the city. Get your families together and get ready for trouble. If you have anywhere else to go, then go. Now. Flee while you can.'

'And the church?' they wanted to know.

'The church will be scattered,' he said sadly. 'It will have to go underground.'

'But you? Where will you go? What will you do?'

'I'll stay here unless the Lord tells me to move on,' he said. 'I have no idea right now what he wants me to do.'

They took him at his word, as they'd always done. The city prepared for Louis's attack; some packed their belongings and fled; others stayed behind and with grim determination prepared for Louis's onslaught.

Within a week John got his orders from God. And they came, strangely enough, by way of King Louis himself. First there was the messenger at the door. As the king's "official minister," John was ordered to leave the city and go to the town of Rochelle!

Before the week was out, horses and wagons (ordered by the king) were drawn up in front of his house, and their belongings were hastily packed and hoisted up on them. John bade the people in his church a sad good-bye. Sixteen years he'd been there, and he'd learned to love them well, and they him. And there were tears and prayers as there had been those many long years ago when he'd knelt on the beach with his family in the early morning hours and said good-bye to their beloved Scotland.

But for John and Elizabeth and their sons, grown now, Rochelle turned out to be only a stopping place. In a matter of a few months, God gave John his marching orders again. This time it was back to the British Isles!

He had long given up hope of ever going back there, but permission came out of the blue. *Back home again*?

Well – almost.

* * *

England is what "back home" turned out to be. Yes! King James I of England* finally gave his permission, and word was sent to the king of France to release Welch and let him go back home! But! King James of England still would not give John permission to return to Scotland.

So John and his family settled in London. And it was a time in their lives when there did not seem to be one gleam of light, not one word from God.

Even John's health and strength forsook him. Some doctors thought he had leprosy; other doctors thought he had been poisoned. Whatever it was, it left him so weak he could hardly move about, much less carry on at the pace he'd been used to all his life.

As if that weren't enough, something very peculiar had been happening to his knees. Those long nights of prayer had taken their toll; his knees had become calcified; they were as hard as the horns of a cow. It rendered him almost incapable of walking. And if he had been able to get around, it would have

---

* *King James VI of Scotland*

done him no good, for he had been forbidden to preach.

Now all this would have been enough to finish off any ordinary Christians. But John and Elizabeth were not ordinary Christians. They had something built into them that wouldn't say "die". They had *nerve* and they had *spirit!*

So the things they did in the latter part of their lives were every bit as exciting and filled with adventure as some of the things they did when they were young!

* * *

Elizabeth hurried along the corridor of the palace of Whitehall in London. It was a huge complex of buildings, some of which the royal family used as their private dwellings; one of them was where you were fortunate enough to get an audience with the king. Elizabeth was. For some of her mother's relatives had connections in the court. And Elizabeth not only had nerve enough to ask for an audience with the king – she had actually gotten an audience.

She hurried along toward her appointment, slim and trim and dressed in her best, her dainty apron and cap made of the finest material and washed as white as snow.

When she was ushered into the huge room, she waited quietly until it was her turn to go forward and be addressed by the king.

When she was called, she stood before him without a sign of fear. He read the information that one of his courtiers had handed him, and the great room was silent, waiting. Then he looked up over the paper to this tiny woman.

'I understand that you are asking for my permission to allow your husband to return to Scotland,' he said in a voice that was meant to scare her out of her wits.

'Yes, Sire,' she answered. 'The physicians tell us that there is no other way to save his life. I beg you to let him go back to his home, to breathe his native air.' She was soft-spoken and respectful, but there was something about her – it was a spark. No – it was a fire!

Clearly this little woman did not scare easily.

She had an inner strength – and not just because she was John Welch's wife, either.

The king leaned back in his chair and studied her in silence. When he spoke, his voice was dry and crackling and bent for trouble.

'Whose daughter are you?' he said. 'I know you are John Welch's wife – but whose *daughter*?'

'I am John Knox's daughter, Sire.' She dropped it like a bombshell. It sent a quiver throughout the whole room.

'Knox and Welch?' the king fairly bellowed, when he finally found his voice. 'Surely the devil never made such a match as that!'

'Indeed he did not, Sire,' she shot back. 'For we never asked his advice!'

The very air in the room seemed to snap, crackle, and pop, as those words danced in the air.

'How many children does your father have?' he said at last, changing the subject. He'd better keep on his toes, he thought, or this little woman was going to get the best of him in front of his entire court. 'Are you the only one?'

'No, Sire, there are three of us.'

'And the other two? Lads or lassies?'

'Lassies, Sire, all three of us.'

He threw up his hands. 'God be thanked!' he cried. 'And if they'd been lads, I'd never have ruled my three kingdoms in peace!'

Now the courtroom was abristle with excitement. Everyone listened. A conversation like this they were not likely to hear again in a hurry!

Now it was Elizabeth who changed the subject – or rather, she got it back on the track. 'I ask you again, Sire – I beg you – to let him go back to his own beloved Scotland. Give him this!'

'Give him the devil!' the king bellowed, really angry now. This woman was making a fool of him. His eyes glared at her triumphantly, as if to say, 'Now I've got you!'

But he was wrong.

'Give the devil to your hungry courtiers,' she shot back, unafraid.

The king leaned back in his chair and stared at her; his eyes were crafty now. He'd fix her, he thought – there must be some way he could send her out in tears. He did not move a muscle, just stared; but the wheels in his head were going around. *Lift her hopes up, then dash them to the ground – that ought to do it.*

'I shall allow your husband to return to Scotland,' he said – '*If...* if you will persuade him to bow down to my bishops.'

Aha! His eyes said. *That'll do it.*

But again he was wrong.

Elizabeth lifted up her apron and held it aloft toward the king. 'Please, Sire,' she said, and her eyes were on fire with triumph. 'I'd rather have his head – right here.'

The king could only stare at her. There was no way he could finish this woman off. She was a tiger, she was, and if he didn't turn tail and run, she'd finish *him* off, right in front of his own court. There was only one thing to do. He nodded to a guard to indicate that the interview was over. He had nothing more to say. He'd been totally unprepared for the fire and the nerve in this woman. She was as unstoppable as her husband!

Elizabeth turned and sailed out of the room, her head held high – and the guards closed the door behind her.

Unstoppable they had been all their lives, and unstoppable they still were.

And their friends!

They were unstoppable too!

They would not give up, but kept pleading with the king to at least let John preach in London. His answer was always a fervent *no*. He knew what was good for *him*. If he ever let John go back to Scotland, he, the king, would not be able to keep his bishops in power. And even if he just let John preach in London, the story would be the same.

The king was beginning to enjoy this little game by now. He played with John's and

Elizabeth's future as a cat plays with a mouse, meaning to torment them to the end.

'And how is Dr Welch's health?' he would inquire innocently. And when his informers would answer that it was worse, he would shake his head, meaning to look sad – and not fooling anybody. This went on for months, while John's condition grew weaker and weaker.

And then the day came when he inquired about John's health and the answer was, 'He's dying, Sire.'

This was the moment the king had been waiting for. This was the moment of his greatest triumph in this little war of nerves. This was the moment when he could get even with the minister and his wife.

'So, then, all hope is past?' he inquired.

'Yes, Sire, all hope is past. The man will be dead within hours.'

'I just wanted to make sure,' the king answered. 'Now, then. I have been thinking this matter over very carefully. And I've decided that perhaps I've been unnecessarily hard on Dr Welch. Therefore, I shall be more lenient. I shall give permission, out of the kindness of my heart, to let him preach anywhere in London he pleases.' His eyes were agleam with triumph, and he licked his chops as he said it.

They bowed, thanked him, and left.

'I've won,' the king thought. 'Let him preach now. Let him preach his heart out!'

And that was when he found out just how unstoppable John and Elizabeth Welch were!

UNSTOPPABLE

It was nearly noon now. Elizabeth was sitting by John's bedside. His sons were standing against the wall, tears streaming down their faces, waiting for their father to die – only in his fifties, but already a broken old man, unable to raise his head; spent, totally spent, for the Lord – his knees as hard as the horns of a cow, calcified from long hours of kneeling through the years, as he talked with his God.

What a father they'd had. What a ball of fire. Their hearts were torn between pride and grief. And why should he die like this – broken, defeated – down in disgrace in his last hours?

And because of a king!

Why their father's king was Christ!

And had Christ himself deserted this warrior, this unstoppable soldier, this man who all his life had been incapable of defeat?

Why, they thought, *why*?

Elizabeth sat, silent. She kept back her tears for their sakes. This unstoppable husband of hers, she thought, was at last going to die in defeat. It was incredible – it seemed impossible – she could not believe it. But it was so. She clung to his hand; he was too weak to cling to hers.

Christ, for whom he had led his life, was going to, at long last, let him down. Why? *Why*?

She could not even pray; she could only cling to his almost lifeless hand.

And then, a knock at the door.

The gloomy little delegation came into the room; they had just been to see the king. And their report was so pitiful, so ironic, that it did nothing to relieve the gloom.

'The king has granted Dr.Welch permission to preach in London,' they said. Their words fell like lead into the gloomy room. The king had triumphed at last; there was no way John could preach now – the king had had the last laugh.

The tears streamed down their faces, and at last Elizabeth broke down in sobs. She let go of John's hand and fished for her handkerchief in her apron pocket. She cried unashamedly. All the strength had gone out of her. And all the hope, and all the fire.

The room was silent, except for the sobbing.

And then there was a flutter of John's eyelids. And a moving of his hands, as they reached out and grabbed the coverlet. And began to push it down!

They stared at him, unbelieving.

And then they *listened*, unbelieving.

'So the king says I can preach?' he said. 'Then I shall preach!'

If an earthquake had hit the house they could not have been more astonished.

'I shall preach,' he repeated, stronger now. 'Is the London lecture hall still available?'

'Yes,' the spokesman for the delegation said. 'It is – but –'

'Then get messengers out,' came the voice from the bed. 'And tell the people I shall be there tonight – and I shall preach.'

Elizabeth's hand shot out in warning, to tuck him back in.

'No, Elizabeth,' he said. 'You have never disobeyed me in all our lives. You cannot disobey me now.' And was there – or did she fancy it – the old twinkle in his eyes – the old fire she knew so well?

She looked at him a long moment. Then turned to the delegation. 'Do as he says,' she said quietly. 'It is his last desire.' *Humour him*, her eyes begged, *there can be no harm in it now*.

They looked at her, incredulous – and turned and left the room.

Within hours there was set in motion the most fanciful, the most pathetic plan that anyone ever dreamed of. The great Dr Welch was going to preach in the London lecture hall that very night. It was impossible; they knew it would fail, but if it was his dying wish, then they would do it.

And they did. The word went out by messengers; Dr Welch would preach.

All London was abuzz with excitement. Were the rumours of Dr Welch's impending death false, after all? Why, he was dying – everyone said so – how could he preach?

* * *

Throughout the day, the messengers kept at their missions, and the tongues wagged.

And throughout the hours, back in John Welch's house, Elizabeth kept her vigil by John's bedside. He lay quiet, but his eyes were open, and they glowed with a strange light. He napped, then woke again, always with the same strange glow in his eyes, then napped again. Was he dreaming? Was he about to die? Elizabeth did not know. The servants brought in nourishment, but she refused it. She just sat there, waiting.

The long afternoon wore on, and evening came. She watched him, afraid to move.

The delegation came back, and filed into his room. 'All has been arranged,' they said. 'It was his dying wish.'

Then, 'is it time?' the voice came from the deathbed.

They did not dare answer. Would he preach, in his fancy, at the last, from his deathbed?

But the dying hands came up, pushed the covers back, and John struggled up on his elbows, then into a sitting position. 'Get me out of here,' he said. 'I'm going to preach.'

The delegation, and his sons, looked at Elizabeth, pleading.

'Help him up,' she said at last. 'It can do no harm now. And help me get him dressed.'

They did, with trembling hands.

And carried him out to a waiting carriage.

And drove him to the London lecture hall!

He will die before he gets there, they thought.

And, *He will die before he gets there*, Elizabeth thought too, as they drove up to the London lecture hall and stopped. *But it is the last, the very last thing I can do for him* – TO LET HIM DIE ON HIS WAY TO PREACH.

But John had more in mind than this.

He had *preaching* in mind, and he was not about to let anyone's unbelief keep him from it. Preach he would – he was sure of it!

He looked out of the carriage window. Outside the London lecture hall – crowds!

Crowds!

He thought of the crowds outside his church back in Ayr. He thought of the time when King Louis had sent his duke and his guards to arrest him. He thought of the street fights back in Kirkcudbright. And all of his youth and all of his fire and all of his strength came back in a rush, like a tidal wave. Preach – he'd done it all his life, and preach he would!

Now!

Now!

NOW!

They took him around to a side door and half led, half carried him, into the lecture hall and up to the lectern.

He was an old man in his fifties, crippled with disease – but his eyes! His eyes!

The great hall grew silent as he was introduced. The people outside crowded in, jammed themselves against the walls. And waited.

The men who were with him helped him up to a standing position. He clung to the lectern and looked out over the worried faces.

He saw again the vast congregation in Ayr. He saw all his life pass before him as he looked. No one – nothing had ever defeated him in all his life.

No one – nothing – would defeat him now!

And he began to preach.

And all the old fire poured forth, out across that great hall – as from a supernatural power, not his own – and their hearts burned within them as they listened.

For an hour, he preached. An hour!

And the power was so great that it shook the very timbers and foundations, just as in the days of old. The very building seemed to be afire!

When he at last finished, the tears were streaming down their faces. And his sons' faces. And Elizabeth's face.

She looked up at him adoringly as she had done through the years, her face glowing with triumph.

When he was finished, he crumpled suddenly, and the men behind him sprang to hold him up. They half carried him out through a side door.

* * *

Back in the Welches' home, the family and a few friends gathered silent. John was back in bed, his body limp, his eyes still glowing. They waited for any word he might have to say. And then it came. But not to them. To God.

'Enough, Lord, enough,' he muttered. 'I can't stand any more joy – I cannot contain it – it is too much.'

And those were the last words he said.

He turned toward Elizabeth in a gesture of love, and she grasped his hand. They looked at each other without words; the memories of all the wonderful years they had spent together passed between them in that last long look.

Then, she picked up the Bible that had lain in her lap, and began to read aloud the words he'd lived by all his life. *The Lord is on my side; I will not fear: what can man do unto me?**

And even as she read, he breathed his last. He had no need now to hear the words read to him; he was in the very presence of God.

---

* *Psalm 118:6 KJV.*

AUTHOR'S NOTE

When telling a story about a person who really lived, the research is only the beginning, the gathering of "facts" often pretty sketchy. They are like a skeleton, to which must be added sinews and muscles and flesh and blood. This is done by inventing incidents and dialogue, to make the story "come alive".

In the case of John Welch, the facts of his life were so incredible that they seem like inventions. Such outlandish adventures could not have really happened! But they did.

John Welch was born about the year 1570. He was by birth a gentleman, for his father was Laird of an estate in Nithsdale, Scotland.

John ran away from home when he was in his early teens and joined a band of thieves on the border of Scotland and England. I hope I'll be forgiven for filling in the possible details of this sojourn. He stayed with the thieves until his clothes were in rags and then went back to his father, stopping at his aunt Agnes Forsythe's house on the way, to beg her to intercede for him. It is true that his father paid a surprise visit while he was there. After his aunt Agnes had pled his case, she admitted that John was in the house, and "called upon him to come to his father." Where she had him hiding is not clear, but it seemed to me that a closet would do nicely for a dramatic hiding place. His father forgave him and John finished his schooling, became a minister, and married Elizabeth Knox of Edinburgh.

All the events of his various pastorates in Scotland are true. His influence on the son of the Mitchelhills in Selkirk is true (I named him Jamie). And in Ayr, the fights, the setting of tables in the middle of the streets, the plague in the horses' packs, and John's arrest and incarceration in prison, followed by his exile in 1606 to France – all true.

His adventures in France are true – including his preaching in French in fourteen weeks, the "resurrection" of the student who had been declared dead, the Catholic friar who thought John was "talking with devils," and the siege of Louis XIII, King of France. Yes, a cannonball pierced his bed, and yes, another knocked the powder ladle out of his hand – only descriptions and dialogue were added.

When John got back to England, the events there were also true. But in this case, so is the unforgettable dialogue between Elizabeth and His

Majesty King James I (King James VI of Scotland)! I perceive John Welch to have been a stern man, but a warm and tender one, for *Scots Worthies* says that "he made no show of his learning," that "his utterance was tender and moving," and that "no man could hear him preach and forebear weeping, his conveyance was so affecting."

The year of his birth was "about the year 1570." And the year of his death is not recorded – only that "he lived a little more than fifty-two years."

What a man. And what a life. It was an exciting adventure just to write about it. I hope it was equally exciting for you to read.

- *Ethel Barrett*

QUIZ

1. In what year was John Welch born?

2. What was his mother's name?

3. What did John do when he was a young boy that was against the fifth and the eighth commandments?

4. What does the word hugger-muggery mean?

5. Where did John's Aunt Agnes live?

6. Can you think of a Bible story that Jesus told which is similar to John's earlier life?

7. What did John want to be then?

8. Name three places in Scotland where John worked.

9. Who did John ask to be his wife?

10. Which other great Scottish reformer was John's wife related to?

11. What disease threatened John's town?

12. Which king imprisoned him?

13. To what country was John banished to?

14. In what town in France did he preach?

15. What disturbed the friar monk from his sleep when he was at the Welch's house?

16. How did King Louis of France almost kill John Welch?

17. What did King Louis do to John Welch after a meeting with him?

18. To what country did the Welches go to next?

19. What king did Elizabeth Welch have a meeting with?

20. In what city did John preach his last sermon?

ANSWERS

1. 1570
2. Marion Grier
3. He ran away from home and joined a band of robbers
4. Confusion
5. Dumfries
6. The Prodigal Son
7. A minister
8. Selkirk, Kirkcudbright and Ayr
9. Elizabeth Knox
10. John Knox
11. The plague
12. James VI of Scotland and I of England
13. France
14. St Jean D'Angely
15. John's praying
16. He made him the official minister to the crown
17. By a cannon ball through the wall of his house which just missed him
18. England
19. James VI of Scotland and I of England
20. London

Ethel Barrett

Ethel Barrett was well known as a speaker, author, lecturer, radio and television personality as well as a Christian educator. She was also a mother to me and my brother Stephen Barrett. She often tried out her new stories on us when we were kids, to see if they worked — which they did!

My mother had Scottish forebears. So when she came across information on the great John Welch she ran with it. She just had to write a book about this amazing Scottish character.

Gary Barrett

JOHN WELCH
TIME LINE

1553	Death of Edward VI, King of England. Lady Jane Grey proclaimed Queen of England. Her reign lasts nine days before she is deposed and Mary I is proclaimed Queen instead.
1554	Execution of Lady Jane Grey.
1555	England returns to Roman Catholicism. Cranmer burned at the stake.
1558	Elizabeth I crowned Queen of England. Repeal of Catholic legislation in England.
1567	Murder of Lord Darnley, husband of Mary Queen of Scots. Mary Queen of Scots forced to abdicate. Her son, James VI, is crowned King of Scotland.
1568	Mary Queen of Scots imprisoned by Elizabeth I at Fotheringay Castle.
1570	John Welch born.
1577	Francis Drake sails round the world.
1587	Mary Queen of Scots executed.
1588	Spanish Armada defeated by the English fleet.
1590	John Welch moves from Kirkudbright to Ayr.

1603	Elizabeth I dies.
	James VI of Scotland is crowned James I of England.
1605	John Welch imprisoned by James I.
	Gun Powder plot. Guy Fawkes and other Roman Catholic conspirators fail in attempt to blow up parliament and the King.
1606	Dutch discover Australia.
	The telescope is invented.
1607	Colony of Virginia is founded.
1610	Hudson Bay discovered.
	Galileo sees Jupiter's moons.
1611	Authorised version of the Bible completed.
1616	William Shakespeare dies.
	The Scottish church sets up schools in every parish to teach children "godliness and knowledge".
1620	Pilgrims land at Plymouth Rock in Cape Cod, Massachusetts in the Mayflower.
1622	John Welch dies aged 52.
1625	James I dies.
	Charles I crowned King of England.
1628	Blood circulation is understood for the first time.
1643	The Taj Mahal is completed in India.
1649	Charles I is imprisoned and executed.
1653	Oliver Cromwell becomes Lord Protector.

JOHN WELCH
SUMMARY

Who was he?

Born into a noble Scottish family, John Welch disobeyed his parents by running away and joining a band of theives. In one way the story of John's early life is very like the story that Jesus told about the Prodigal Son in Luke chapter 15. However, he eventually went on to become a great preacher and reformer and married the daughter of another Scottish reformer, John Knox. John Welch was born round about the year 1570. His father John Welch of Collieston in Nithsdale was a wealthy land owner in the Borders of Scotland. His mother was Marian Grier Welch. His aunt lived in Dumfries.

Ministerial Work

His first ministerial charge was in Selkirk. He then moved to Kirkcudbright. In the year 1590 he moved to Ayr.

Adventures

In 1605 John Welch was imprisoned by King James I of England and VI of Scotland. In the year 1606 John sailed from the docks at Leith to a new life in France.

Death

He died in London at the age of 52.

JOHN KNOX
SUMMARY

Who was he?
John Knox was an influential Protestant reformer. He was born at Haddington in East Lothian in 1505. His father was William Knox.

Education
At sixteen he went to Glasgow University and then to St. Andrews where he met George Wishart who persuaded him to become a protestant. In 1548 St Andrews was captured and Knox was forced into serving as a galley slave on a French ship. It is believed that King Edward VI of England interceded and secured his release.

Life
He lived during a time of great political change. He made loyal friends and fierce enemies — one of which was Mary Queen of Scots. The Protestant religion he supported was recognised in the year 1590.

Death
When dying he asked his wife to read aloud the seventeenth chapter of John's gospel. This was the part of the Bible that had first persuaded him to trust in Jesus Christ. He died November 24, 1572

SCOTLAND SUMMARY

Scotland's size, population and location
Scotland is 78,772 square kilometres, 440 kilometres long and 248 kilometres wide. The coastline is so rugged and indented that its total length is estimated to be 3,680 kilometres. In 1991 its population was about 5,100,000. Scotland is in the north of the British Isles. It is bounded west and north by the Atlantic and on the east by the North Sea. It borders with England in the south.

The origins of Scotland's name
The name "Scotland" comes from the Scoti, a Celtic tribe who migrated to Scotland from Ireland during the fifth and sixth centuries.

Scotland's Mountains
They are not as high as in the rest of Europe but have the highest mountain peak in the United Kingdom (Ben Nevis 1,356 metres).

Scotland's climate
Despite how far North it is, Scotland's climate is remarkably mild due to the warm Gulf Stream from the South Atlantic. However snow, ice and falling temperatures can make conditions dangerous on higher ground during winter months.

History — Romans

The Romans never conquered Scotland but to contain the northern tribes, or Picts, they built two fortified walls. The first was known as Hadrian's Wall. The second was the Antonine Wall. The Roman Empire itself collapsed after AD 350. Later, in about AD 580, St Columba set out to bring the gospel to the King of the Picts.

History — Struggles and Conflict

There was much mistrust between Scotland and England throughout Scotland's history. The two nations were at war, on and off, for 700 years. Then in the 16th century a lengthy religious struggle began between the Protestants and the Roman Catholic church.

In 1603 Scotland and England were joined by the same King when James VI of Scotland became also James I of England upon the death of Queen Elizabeth I. In 1707 legislation was passed that united the two Parliaments.

However in 1745 Charles Stuart tried to regain the British throne for the House of Stuart. His troops were crushed at the Battle of Culloden in April 1746.

On this map you can see the three countries that John Welch lived in as well as other European countries as they exist today. The capital of England and the United Kingdom is the city of London; this is also where John Welch died. The map of Europe is continually changing. One difference here is that in John Welch's time Italy was not yet a unitied country.

On this map you can see the Western Isles on one coast and the North Sea on the other. Note the different places that John would have been familiar with - these are all situated in what would now be referred to as The Central Belt or Lowlands. On this map it is referred to as The Borders because this area is the border between Scotland and England. On the East Coast you can see the city of Edinburgh, the capital of Scotland.

Here we have a map of France. On this map you can see the coastal
waters in the North that separate France from the United Kingdom -
this is called The English Channel or La Manche if you live in France.
The capital city is Paris and Calais is one of its main coastal ports. If
you are travelling from the United Kingdom to France you can take a
ferry from Dover to Calais or travel by train in an underground tunnel.
La Rochelle and St Jean-d'Angely are the two French towns that we
hear about during John Welch's life in France.

WHAT WAS LIFE LIKE THEN?

Before the Reformation — during the period we call The Middle Ages which started after the end of the Roman Empire and finished at the end of the 1500's - life was very different to what we know now. If you went to school it was most likely that you were taught in a monastery – a big building where priests and monks lived and worked. You would have lived, slept and studied there – so it was a bit like a boarding school is today.

You would normally only get an education if you belonged to a wealthy family but sometimes monastaries took in young boys from poorer families. They taught them reading, writing and arithmetic. Places were limited and they would only take the most gifted children – and never girls.

Textbooks were very rare so in order to learn things you used a slate and a pencil to write things down. You spent a lot of time memorising facts.

However, if you were a girl it was very different. Girls from wealthy families were not sent away to school. Daughters of the aristocracy were taught at home. Their families would ensure that they were taught by the best and most respected scholars.

If your father was a well-off merchant you might be sent to a convent for your education. However, if you were from a poor family there was no chance of any education outside the home. All you were taught was how to spin, sew, cook and manage a household.

If you were fortunate enough to attend school, you had to work really hard. To get to class on time you had to get up really early and then your lessons would not be finished until late evening. If you were late or your work wasn't good enough your teacher would give you a beating. Erasmus (a great scholar born in Holland) wrote: "Unless I am there before roll is called I will get a hiding. Not the slightest danger on that score. I was there at just half-past five."

We take many things for granted today. Girls and boys are allowed to study reading, writing and arithmetic, as well as other lessons such as sciences, languages, technology and the arts. Books used to be luxury items for the rich. Nowadays there are even books for babies. We can buy books, borrow them from libraries or read them online on our computers.

Life was tough in the 1500's and on into the 1600's. During the 1600's, or seventeenth century as it is called, the average person lived to only 35 years of age. Most people worked in agriculture (over 67%) and their average working hours were

80 hours a week. A farm labourer received two shillings a week and a loaf of bread cost two pence.

Population figures were very approximate but the population of the world at that time is judged to be about 545,000,000 people. The population of the United Kingdom was 4,800,000 people (or 8% of the world population) and London had a population of 200,000 people (4% of the UK). Scotland's population in 1600 was 800,000 and this increased to 1,000,000 by the year 1707.

We have many things to thank God for. We can read God's word for oursleves and worship God freely and for that and many other changes in schools and churches and our day-to-day lives we owe a lot to people like John Knox and John Welch.

DANGER
ON THE HILL
CATHERINE MACKENZIE

Torchbearers
Danger On The Hill
by C. Mackenzie

"Run, run for your lives," a young boy screamed. "Run, everybody, run. The soldiers are here."

That day on the hill is the beginning of a new and terrifying life for the three Wilson children. Margaret, Agnes and Thomas are not afraid to stand up for what they believe in, but it means that they are forced to leave their home and their parents for a life of hiding on the hills.

If you were a covenanter in the 1600s you were the enemy of the King and the authorities. But all you really wanted to do was worship God in the way he told you to in the Bible. Margaret wants to give Jesus Christ the most important place in her life, and this conviction might cost her life. **There is danger on the hill for Margaret. There is danger everywhere - if you are a covenanter.** The Torchbearers series are true life stories from history where Christians have suffered and died for their faith in Christ.

ISBN I 85792 7842

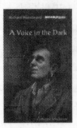

Trailblazers

LIGHT KEEPERS

Start collecting this series now!

**Ten boys who
changed the world**
David Livingstone, Billy Graham,
Brother Andrew, John Newton, William Carey,
George Müller, Nicky Cruz,
Eric Liddell, Luis Palau, Adoniram Judson.

**Ten boys who
made a difference**
Augustine of Hippo,
Jan Hus, Martin Luther,
Ulrich Zwingli, William Tyndale,
Hugh Latimer, John Calvin,
John Knox, Lord Shaftesbury,
Thomas Chalmers.

**Ten boys who
made history**
Charles Spurgeon, Jonathan Edwards,
Samuel Rutherford, D L Moody,
Martin Lloyd Jones, A W Tozer, John Owen,
Robert Murray McCheyne, Billy Sunday,
George Whitfield.

LIGHT KEEPERS

Start collecting this series now!

Ten girls who
changed the world
Corrie Ten Boom, Mary Slessor, Joni Eareckson
Tada, Isobel Kuhn, Amy Carmichael,
Elizabeth Fry, Evelyn Brand, Gladys Aylward,
Catherine Booth, Jackie Pullinger

Ten girls who
made a difference
Monica of Thagaste
Catherine Luther, Susanna Wesley,
Ann Judson, Maria Taylor,
Susannah Spurgeon, Bethan Lloyd-Jones,
Edith Schaeffer, Sabina Wurmbrand,
Ruth Bell Graham.

Ten girls who
made history
Ida Scudder, Betty Green, Jeanette Li,
Mary Jane Kinnaird, Bessie Adams, Emma Dryer,
Lottie Moon, Florence Nightingale,
Heanrietta Mears,
Elisabeth Elliot.

RAIN FOREST
Adventures

Horace Banner

AMAZON
Adventures

Horace Banner

AFRICAN
Adventures

Dick Anderson

Rainforest Adventures and Amazon Adventures by Horace Banner

The Amazon Rainforest is the oldest and largest rain forest in the world. Covering a huge area of South America it has the most varied plant and animal habitat on the planet. Read this book and you will join an expedition into the heart of the rain forest.

Discover the tree Frog's nest, the chamelon who can change it's colour and the very hungry piranha fish. Even the possum can teach a lesson about speaking out for Jesus Christ and the parasol ant can show us how to keep going and not give up. Then there's the brightly coloured toucan whose call reminds us that with God we can do anything. Discover what its like to actually live in the Rain forest. Join in the adventures and experience the exciting and dangerous life of a pioneer missionary in South America.

Rainforest Adventures: ISBN: 1-85792-627-7
Amazon Adventures: ISBN 1-85792-440-1
Look out for African Adventures: ISBN: 1-85972-807-5

CHRISTIAN FOCUS

Staying faithful - Reaching out!

Christian Focus Publications publishes books for adults and children under its three main imprints: Christian Focus, Mentor and Christian Heritage. Our books reflect that God's word is reliable and Jesus is the way to know him, and live for ever with him.

Our children's publication list includes a Sunday school curriculum that covers pre-school to early teens; puzzle and activity books. We also publish personal and family devotional titles, biographies and inspirational stories that children will love.

If you are looking for quality Bible teaching for children then we have an excellent range of Bible story and age specific theological books.

From pre-school to teenage fiction, we have it covered!

Find us at our web page:
www.christianfocus.com